MORE BIBLE TIME WITH KIDS

MORE BIBLE TIME

with Kids

200+
Bible-based
Activities to
Use with
Children

CINDY DINGWALL

Abingdon Press
Nashville

MORE BIBLE TIME WITH KIDS
200 + BIBLE-BASED ACTIVITIES TO USE WITH CHILDREN

Copyright © 2006 by Cindy Dingwall

This book is printed on acid-free paper.

Library of Congress Cataloging-in-Publication Data

Dingwall, Cindy.
    More Bible time with kids : 200 + Bible-based activities to use with children / Cindy Dingwall.
        p. cm.
    Includes bibliographical references (p.   ) and index.
    ISBN 0-687-49230-0 (binding: pbk., adhesive : alk. paper)
    1. Games in Christian education. 2. Bible games and puzzles. 3. Christian education of children. 4. Church work with children. 5. Bible—Study and teaching (Primary)—Activity programs. I. Title.

BV1536.3.D56 2006
268'.432—dc22

2006006910

06 07 08 09 10 11 12 13 14 15—10 9 8 7 6 5 4 3 2 1

MANUFACTURED IN THE UNITED STATES OF AMERICA

To my friend Anne Glabe,
who shares my love of the Lord!

Contents

Acknowledgments

Many thanks to:

The Reverend Michael Morris, Senior Pastor of First United Methodist Church in Palatine, Illinois, for praying with me about this project.

Erick McKnight, Director of Children's Ministries at First United Methodist Church in Palatine, Illinois, for answering my questions during the preparation of this book.

The wonderful ladies in Dorcas Circle for their prayers and good wishes.

The staff at Prospect Heights Public Library in Prospect Heights, Illinois, for their ongoing support and encouragement as I created this book. Special thanks go to Alice Johnson and Betty Shubeck for sharing ideas, and to Sue Seggeling who reminded me that I would get this book finished on time.

To my friends who always tell me to "keep on going!" Thank you to Carolyn O'Donnell for our weekly lunches that nourish my body and the time away that refreshes my creativity.

To my wonderful Westie, Tara, who takes me for daily walks and snuggles by my feet as I create and write.

Introduction

More Bible Time with Kids is packed with exciting adventures that will help children learn Bible stories and the lessons they teach. In this book you will find an abundance of creative ideas for sharing Bible stories with children in grades kindergarten through fifth. Storytelling, creative dramatics, puppetry, music, crafts, games, puzzles, bulletin boards, and more help to bring the Bible stories alive. Key verses are listed for each Bible story. Memorizing the key verses can help the children remember the Bible story. Provide small prizes for children who memorize Bible verses.

Consider featuring each of these Bible stories for congregational worship. The service can revolve around the Bible story, and children can be invited to share a song, puppet show, or dramatization during worship. A "Worship Tie-in" is suggested with each lesson.

You'll find three *Sonsational* Sunday Celebrations in this book. These are patterned after popular fun fairs, which kids enjoy, with the added benefit of a Christian theme. Parents are invited to attend these programs with their children so they can develop an understanding of what their children are learning. They incorporate several weeks of study into a fun fair program where kids and parents "travel" to different booths that engage them in a wide variety of enjoyable learning activities.

The "All Year Long" section features social and service activities for the entire church family. There is also a bulletin board idea for each month. Encourage all church members to participate in the service project included with each month's activities.

At the end of the book, you'll find a section called "Bible Activities." Here you will find three activities, three games, and three art projects that encompass all of the Bible stories included in this book.

The lessons have been designed so that activities flow naturally, so try to follow each lesson plan as presented. Feel free, however, to adapt the activities to the ages and abilities of the children in your group.

More Bible Time with Kids can be used in Sunday schools, Christian schools, home-school programs, church camps, after-school programs, and vacation Bible school. Now, go into the world and share God's love with the children you teach!

Before You Begin

Making Christian education programs an enjoyable and valuable experience for children and teachers can be challenging at best. Today's children are bombarded with so much media that traditional programs tend to be boring and mundane. We need to do all we can to entice children to learn about the Lord. Use the following ideas to begin making your program more interesting.

Give your program an exciting name, something other than Sunday school. For example, call your program "Celebration Station." The teachers can be referred to as Station Masters. Give cool names to the different age groups of kids (Engineers, Commuters, Conductors, Agents). Devise clever names for your vacation Bible school, after-school, and midweek programs (Rush Hour Express, Gateway to God).

Make a large weatherproof sign that says CELEBRATION STATION. Hang it outside the building by the entrance closest to where your Christian education program meets. If this sign can be designed so it lights up, all the better. Create an eye-catching sign that frames the doorway leading into your Christian education area. If necessary, make this so it can be put up and taken down as needed during the week.

Make attractive signs to hang outside the door to each room. Label them according to the age groups (Engineers, Conductors, Commuters, Agents).

If the name Celebration Station doesn't work for your group, brainstorm with your director of Christian education and your education committee to come up with another catchy name such as Jericho Junction, Promised Land, or The Village.

Let the teachers and kids dress in Bible costumes for some of the lessons. Inexpensive costumes can be purchased after Halloween in party stores and costume shops. Other costumes can be easily made from sturdy fabrics. Take a long rectangle of fabric, fold it in half lengthwise, cut out a triangular opening for the head, and slip it over the person's body. Tie it at the waist with rope.

Set up your teaching area so it goes with the story you are teaching. See each lesson for ideas for room setups. Ask artistic people in your congregation to paint generic Bible backgrounds to go with your lessons (for example, outdoor scenes, insides of homes, inside the tabernacle). These backgrounds will work for many lessons. Make these out of plywood and put hinges on them, so they can be easily folded up and stored away. You can add *set pieces* to your backgrounds (for example, large boulders, large potted plants, simple rustic furniture, rugs).

When sharing the Bible story, use the books listed in the "Something Special" section or present a flannel board version of the story. Bring in props to use in telling Bible stories. Use puppets and stuffed animals. When presented in an interesting way, the stories will capture the children's interest. The books in the "Something Special" sections can be found in many public libraries or Christian bookstores. You can add them to your church library by establishing a Birthday Book Club. Ask church members to donate money to the church on their birthdays, and use that money to purchase books for your program. Put a bookplate inside each book to let people know who donated the books.

You can create your own flannel boards or purchase them at Christian bookstores. See the Suppliers Guide in the back of this book for companies that make and sell these flannel boards.

If you cannot find suitable books or flannel boards to highlight the stories, ask members of the congregation to dress in costume and present a short dramatization of the story to the children. Ask your youth group to create puppets for a story and present it as a puppet show.

If you have children's librarians in your congregation, enlist their assistance. They are creative people who know how to make story sharing exciting through the use of props, flannel boards, puppetry, and more. Visit your public library and become acquainted with the children's librarians. They possess a wealth of knowledge about children's materials and creative ways to share stories with kids. Given ample time and opportunity, these people will be able to provide much assistance to you.

Teachers and park district employees can also bring an abundance of creative ideas and energy to your program.

Begin planning early. This allows you time to gather the materials you need and plan how you want to teach each lesson. Have all of your materials prepared and ready to go *before* the children arrive. Arrive at church 30 to 60 minutes ahead of time, so you have time to set up your teaching area, prepare your materials, get your craft project ready to go, and so on.

Always prepare a sample of the craft ahead of time, so you know how to demonstrate making it for the children.

Be ready and waiting to greet the children *before* they arrive at church.

Section One

SOME AMAZING ADVENTURES

The Bible is filled with some amazing adventures of people who faced challenges and struggles. By relying on God's grace to give them strength and courage, these people overcame their challenges and deepened their faith in the Lord.

These stories can be shared at any time of the year, however you need to choose a block of at least seven weeks to enjoy them. Spend a week or two with each lesson. When you have completed all six lessons, you and the children, along with their parents, can celebrate with a *Sonsational* Sunday Celebration. Everyone can participate in an Amazing Adventures program that is explained on pages 36-40.

The Amazing Adventures program will combine the six stories into a fun fair program that will reinforce what you and the children have learned. It will bring parents and children together, so they can learn together and share some family time learning about the courage and strength God gives us. Parents and children can be encouraged to discuss what they have learned.

Encourage parents and children to ask questions that will engage them in a discussion of how God gives us strength and courage to face challenges in our lives.

Now, go forth and share some Amazing Adventures together, and as you make your journey through these lessons, reflect upon the awesome love of our Creator.

THE TOWER OF BABEL

Offer this program at any time of the year. Set up the room to look like a construction zone. Put up yellow caution tape and yellow signs that say Construction Zone, Caution, and People Working. Set out construction tools, bricks, hard hats, wheelbarrows.

SCRIPTURE: GENESIS 11

Key Verse (Genesis 11:6): "And the LORD said, 'Look, they are one people, and they have all one language; and this is only the beginning of what they will do; nothing that they propose to do will now be impossible for them.'"

THEME

We need to focus on glorifying God in all we do. God is pleased when all of our acts glorify God, and things work out for the best. We should honor and pray to God, not false gods.

SOMETHING SPECIAL

Read this book to the children:
   The Tower of Babel by Marilyn Hirsh

DISCUSSION

Ask the children if all of the people in the world speak the same language. What are some of the languages other people speak? Do you know how to speak another language? Do you know people who speak other languages? Explain that this was God's way of having people speak different languages. Ask why God decided that people should speak different languages.

Talk about the tower itself. Explain that it was built like a pyramid (show them pictures of pyramids). It was called a ziggurat (ZIG-er-at). It had stairs on the outside of the tower. There was a temple on top of the building. Ziggurats were about 300 feet high, and they were very wide. These towers were easily seen in the cities. *The Life Application Bible* has a good explanation of how the tower was built. Share this with the children.

Tell the children that the people were building this tower to honor themselves rather than to honor God. The people would climb to the top of the tower where they would offer prayers to false gods. They did not pray to the real God. Was this a good thing or a bad thing to do? What do you think God thought about their tower? Discuss the importance of doing things that honor God. How can we honor God? We should never pray to false gods or honor false gods. Who or what are false gods? Why should we pray only to God and not false gods?

IDEA

Ask several people in your congregation who are fluent in a variety of different languages to visit your class. Let them say the Lord's Prayer in a language other than English. Then ask them all to say the Lord's Prayer in that language at the same time.

See how the children react. Tell them that's what God hears every day. "God hears even more languages than what we just heard and can sort it all out and understand each and every language that is being spoken, even when people are all talking at the same time! Isn't *that* awesome!" Ask the children how they would feel if they were in a room full of people who were all talking at once, plus they were all talking in different languages. Would you be able to figure it out? (Probably not, but God sure can!)

ACTIVITY: LET'S BUILD A TOWER

Instructions are on page 3.

 SONG

"They're Building a Tower" (*"The Farmer in the Dell"*)

They're building a tower. They're building a tower.
Hey! Hey! Up it goes. They're building a tower!

Look it's getting tall! Look it's getting tall!
Hey! Hey! Up it goes. They're building a tower!

God took a look and said, God took a look and said,
"Hey! Hey! Look at them. I wonder what is next?"

God sent them all away. God sent them all away.
Hey! Hey! Listen now. Listen to them speak!

 CRAFT: TOWER OF BABEL TIC-TAC-TOE GAME

Instructions are on pages 3-4.

 BULLETIN BOARD: A TOWER TO THE LORD

Instructions are on page 4.

 WORSHIP TIE-IN: TOWERS FOR GOD

Display the towers created by the children in the sanctuary. Invite the children to sing "They're Building a Tower" for congregational worship.

 ACTIVITY: LET'S BUILD A TOWER

MATERIALS
Lots and lots of building blocks (wooden, Lego, Duplo)

DIRECTIONS
- Let the kids build their own Towers of Babel with blocks. Divide the class into groups, and see who can build the biggest and best tower. Tell the children that their towers will be unlike the Tower of Babel, because "we will build our towers to honor the Lord, our God."
- Have one group build a tower without speaking. If you have children who are bilingual, put them into one group and have each of them speak a language other than English while building the tower. Have another group of children build the tower while speaking English. Ask the entire class to work together to build a gigantic tower. If possible, keep the towers and display them where the congregation can view them. Take digital photos of the towers and put them on your church website.
- Ask members of your congregation who speak different languages to join your class in this activity. As the children are building towers, have your visitors speak the other languages so the children can hear what "Babel" sounds like.

CRAFT: TOWER OF BABEL TIC-TAC-TOE GAME

MATERIALS
One dark brown foam triangle per child
One beige foam square per child
Black permanent markers
Nine blue stones and nine red stones per child
One large resealable plastic bag per child
Several small foam religious symbols per child (cross, heart, star)
Glue

PREPARATION

- Use black marker to draw a tic-tac-toe board on each beige foam square.
- Make one activity packet per child: put the foam square, the foam triangle, and the religious symbols into the plastic bags. Put nine red stones and nine blue stones into each bag.

DIRECTIONS

- Tell the children to remove the foam triangle and foam square from their bags. Have them glue the foam square to the foam triangle. The tic-tac-toe grid must be showing.
- Tell the children to remove the religious symbols from their bags and glue these around the outside edges of their triangles. Put the tic-tac-toe games back into the plastic bags.
- Explain that once these are dry the children can use them to play tic-tac-toe.
- Have some pre-made samples to show the children. Let them use these to play tic-tac-toe in class. Have them play while speaking English; have them play without speaking at all. If you have students who are bilingual, let each of them speak their other language while playing. For example, a Chinese-speaking child could play with a Spanish-speaking child.

 BULLETIN BOARD: A TOWER TO THE LORD

MATERIALS

Different shades of brown paper
Light blue paper
Bright yellow paper

Two plastic straws
Black markers

Pushpins
Clear book tape

PREPARATION

- Cover the bulletin board with blue paper.
- Cut bricks of different shapes and sizes out of the brown paper.
- Make a triangular flag out of the yellow paper, and print the memory verse on it.
- Attach the flag to the straw.

DIRECTIONS

- Give each child a brick and a black marker. Tell them to write something good that they would like to do to honor God: pray, help someone, share, visit someone who is sick.
- Use pushpins to attach the bricks to the board, so they look like a tower.
- Attach the flag to the top of the tower.

BULLETIN BOARD ILLUSTRATION

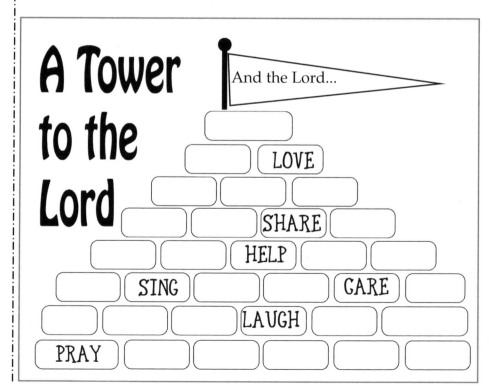

BONUS PUZZLE: CAN YOU BUILD A TOWER?

Use a brown crayon to color all of the bricks that have the word *God* printed on them. When you are finished, you will find a special message.

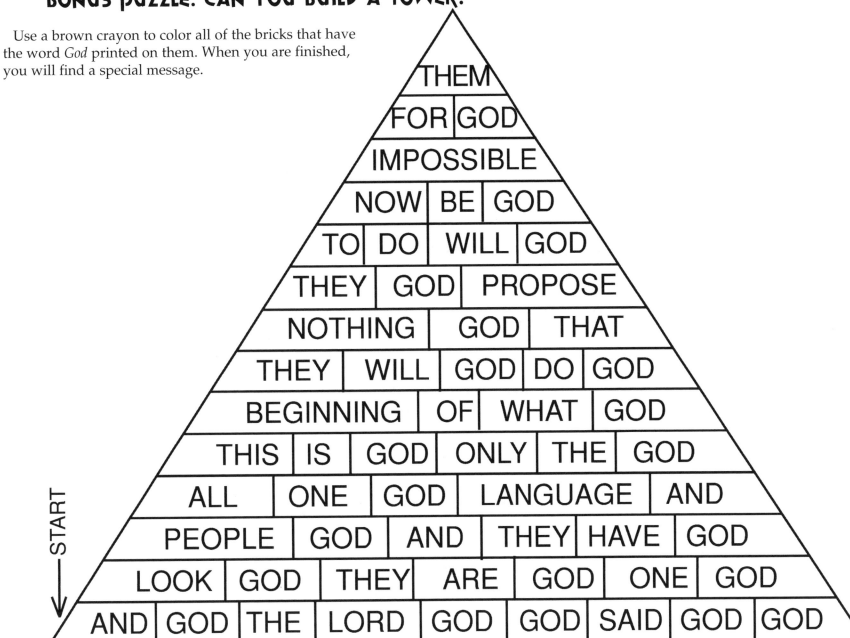

THEM

FOR | GOD

IMPOSSIBLE

NOW | BE | GOD

TO | DO | WILL | GOD

THEY | GOD | PROPOSE

NOTHING | GOD | THAT

THEY | WILL | GOD | DO | GOD

BEGINNING | OF | WHAT | GOD

THIS | IS | GOD | ONLY | THE | GOD

ALL | ONE | GOD | LANGUAGE | AND

PEOPLE | GOD | AND | THEY | HAVE | GOD

LOOK | GOD | THEY | ARE | GOD | ONE | GOD

AND | GOD | THE | LORD | GOD | GOD | SAID | GOD | GOD

START

BONUS PUZZLE SOLUTION: CAN YOU BUILD A TOWER?

Use a brown crayon to color all of the bricks that have the word *God* printed on them. When you are finished, you will find a special message.

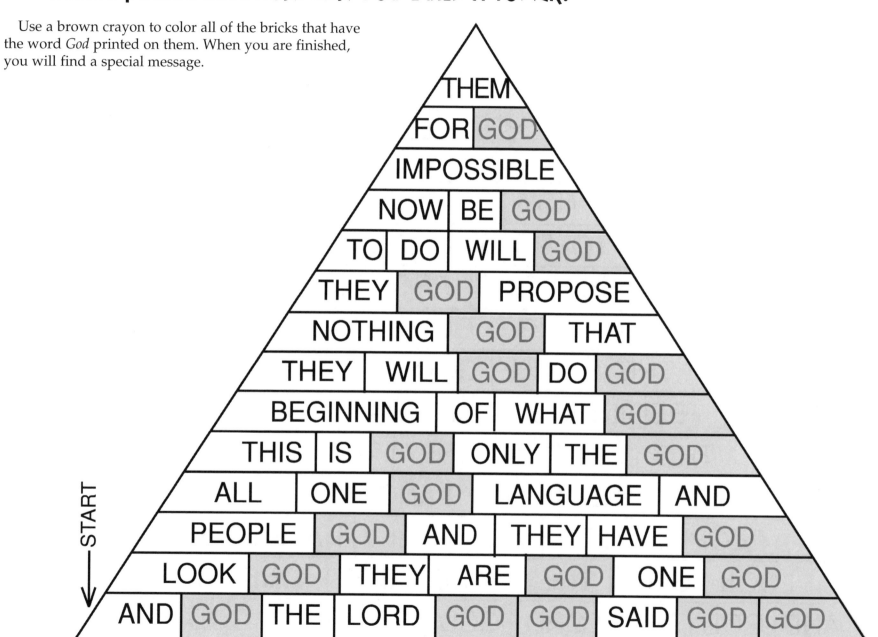

THEM

FOR | GOD

IMPOSSIBLE

NOW | BE | GOD

TO | DO | WILL | GOD

THEY | GOD | PROPOSE

NOTHING | GOD | THAT

THEY | WILL | GOD | DO | GOD

BEGINNING | OF | WHAT | GOD

THIS | IS | GOD | ONLY | THE | GOD

ALL | ONE | GOD | LANGUAGE | AND

PEOPLE | GOD | AND | THEY | HAVE | GOD

LOOK | GOD | THEY | ARE | GOD | ONE | GOD

AND | GOD | THE | LORD | GOD | GOD | SAID | GOD | GOD

START

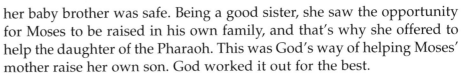

THE BABY IN A BASKET

Offer this program at any time of the year. You'll need a large basket, a baby blanket, and a baby doll. Wrap the doll in the blanket and place it in the basket. Lay a long blue tarp along the floor so it looks like a river. Place the basket into the river. Place a bunch of plants along the riverbanks so it looks like the basket is in the bulrushes. Try to get a recording of a crying baby. Hide the player with the recording so the kids cannot see it, but make sure they can hear it. Let them enter the room to find "a crying baby nestled in a basket among the bulrushes." Have several women from your congregation dress as and portray Miriam, Moses' mother, and the Egyptian women. They can act out the story as you share it.

 ## SCRIPTURE: EXODUS 2:1-10

Key Verse (Exodus 2:4): "His sister stood at a distance, to see what would happen to him."

 ## THEME

God has a way of working things out for the best. We need to trust that God knows what is best for everyone.

 ## SOMETHING SPECIAL

Read either of these books to the children:
Moses in the Bulrushes by Mary Auld
The Baby in the Basket by Jennifer Rees Larcombe

 ## DISCUSSION

Before sharing this story with the children, read the commentary in *The Life Application Bible,* so you will have a better understanding of why Moses' mother had to hide him and later give him up. Explain this to the children and assure them that Moses' mother did this because she loved him. Miriam stood at the riverbank and watched to make sure that her baby brother was safe. Being a good sister, she saw the opportunity for Moses to be raised in his own family, and that's why she offered to help the daughter of the Pharaoh. This was God's way of helping Moses' mother raise her own son. God worked it out for the best.

Ask the children how they think Moses' mother felt when she had to give him up. If you or your assistants have children, share how you would feel if you were Moses' mom.

The children may bring up the fact that some parents give up their children for adoption. If so, explain that sometimes parents cannot take good care of their babies, so they give them up for adoption. That way their children can be raised in a good home where they will be well cared for. Again, this is God's way of working things out. Others may ask what happens to children whose parents die. Again, tell them that parents make sure there will be someone to care for their children if this happens.

 ## SONG

"The Baby in the Basket" (*"The Bear Went Over the Mountain"*)
She put him into the basket; she put him into the basket;
She put him into the basket, and let him float away.
She let him float away; she let him float away.
She put him into the basket, and let him float away.

The baby was found by a slave; the baby was found by a slave;
The baby was found by a slave who wasn't sure what to do.
She wasn't sure what to do; she wasn't sure what to do.
The baby was found by a slave who wasn't sure what to do.

She gave him back to his sister; she gave him back to his sister;
She gave him back to his sister so his mother could take care of him.
So his mother could take care of him, so his mother could take care of
    him.
She gave him back to his sister so his mother could take care of him.

His mother raised her own baby; his mother raised her own baby;
His mother raised her own baby, but then had to give him up.
But then had to give him up, but then had to give him up.
His mother raised her own baby, but then had to give him up.

GAME: WHERE IS MOSES?

Instructions are on page 8.

CRAFT: BABY IN A BASKET

Instructions are on pages 8-9.

ACTIVITY

Let the children tell the story in their own words using the flannel board pieces.

BULLETIN BOARD: A BASKET FILLED WITH LOVE

Instructions are on page 9.

WORSHIP TIE-IN: HIS OWN MOTHER

Have the adults who helped you dramatize this story for the children present this as a pulpit drama for congregational worship. Invite the children to sing the song "The Baby in the Basket" (p. 7).

GAME: WHERE IS MOSES?

MATERIALS

One small basket with a baby doll inside it

DIRECTIONS

• Have the kids sit in a circle and sing "Where Is Moses" (*"Frère Jacques"*).

Where is Moses? Where is Moses?
Do you know? Do you know?
Can you find Moses? Can you find Moses?
And bring him home? And bring him home?

• One child should stand in the center and be *Miriam*.
• Another child should stand off to the side and be the mother of Moses.
• As the children sing, they should close their eyes and wave their arms in the air to make the bulrushes. While they are singing and waving their arms with their eyes closed, Moses' mother should walk around the outside of the group, and place the basket behind one child.
• The children then open their eyes and try to guess where the basket is hidden. The child who guesses correctly becomes Miriam.

CRAFT: BABY IN A BASKET

MATERIALS

½ of an empty walnut shell per child
One miniature plastic baby boy doll per child
One small empty aluminum loaf tin per child
Dirt
One envelope of grass seed and popcorn kernels per child
Glue gun with glue sticks
One small piece of fabric per child
One plastic spoon per child

DIRECTIONS

• Give each child an empty loaf tin, a spoon, and some dirt. Let the children spoon dirt into their loaf tins. They should fill the loaf tin almost to the top.
• Give each child an envelope of grass seed and popcorn kernels. Let them sprinkle the grass and popcorn kernels into the dirt. Push the popcorn kernels deeply into the dirt.
• Give each child an empty walnut shell and a piece of cloth. Help them use the glue guns to glue the *blanket* into the shell.

- Give each child a *baby Moses* doll. Have them glue the dolls inside the shells, wrap the blanket around Moses, and glue it shut.
- Place the basket with baby Moses onto the top of the dirt in the loaf tin.
- Tell the kids to water the dirt and keep it moist. The grass and popcorn should start to grow soon. When the grass seeds and popcorn kernels grow taller, it will look like baby Moses is in the bulrushes.

BULLETIN BOARD: A BASKET FILLED WITH LOVE

MATERIALS

One large piece of blue, fadeless paper to cover the bulletin board
Brown paper in two shades
Red paper
Green paper
Letter stencils (use die-cutting machine if available)
Pushpins
One baby picture of each child

PREPARATION

- Cover the board with blue, fadeless paper.
- Cut out the title A BASKET FILLED WITH LOVE from the red paper and attach it to the board.
- Cut the brown paper into strips, and weave it into a large basket. Attach the basket to the bulletin board.
- Ask each child to bring a baby picture.
- Cut the green paper to look like bulrushes, and attach them to the board.

DIRECTIONS

- Let the children attach their pictures to the bulletin board so it looks like they are nestled in the basket.

BULLETIN BOARD ILLUSTRATION

BONUS PUZZLE: WHAT DID HIS NAME MEAN?

Read the sentence below. It sure doesn't make much sense, does it? See what you can do to help us figure out what it really says.

I RAN **M**OTHER BANANA SISTER DREW BR**O**THER CHERRY HIM LOVE FATHER LI**S**TEN OUT AUNT TURKEY LORD CAN OF UNCLE TH**E** COU**S**IN FAN CHOCOLATE WATER GRANDMOTHER PIE GRANDFATHER.

First, print the boldfaced letters here.

___ ___ ___ ___ ___

Next
Cross out the words that end with the letter N.
Cross out the words that are names of family members.
Cross out words that are foods.
Cross out words that begin with the letter L.
Now print the left over words here to find out what his name means.

___ ___ ___ ___ ___ ___ ___

___ ___ ___ ___ ___ ___ ___

___ ___ ___ ___ ___.

BONUS PUZZLE SOLUTION: WHAT DID HIS NAME MEAN?

Read the sentence below. It sure doesn't make much sense, does it? See what you can do to help us figure out what it really says.

I ~~RAN~~ **M**~~OTHER BANANA SISTER~~ DREW ~~BR**O**THER CHERRY~~ HIM ~~LOVE FATHER~~ LI**S**~~TEN~~ OUT ~~AUNT TURKEY LORD CAN~~ OF ~~UNCLE~~ TH**E** ~~COU**S**IN FAN CHOCOLATE~~ WATER ~~GRANDMOTHER PIE GRANDFATHER~~.

First, print the boldface letters here:

M   O   S   E   S

Next
Cross out the words that end with the letter N.
Cross out the words that are names of family members.
Cross out words that are foods.
Cross out words that begin with the letter L.
Now print the left over words here to find out what his name means.

I   DREW   HIM
OUT   OF   THE
WATER.

Color the picture of Moses in the bulrushes below.

ONE BIG GIANT (DAVID AND GOLIATH)

Offer this program at any time of the year. Create "Goliath," and have him standing in a corner of the room. Use your imagination for this and have fun with it. Find or make a large round piñata and decorate it to look like Goliath's head. Fill the piñata with candy and other prizes. Read the description of Goliath in the Bible story and go from there in creating your own special version of Goliath. Build a frame for the body with long pieces of wood. Use large brown trash bags, paper, yarn, and more to create a really big, scary-looking giant.

SCRIPTURE: 1 SAMUEL 17

Key Verse (1 Samuel 17:37): "Go and may the LORD be with you!"

THEME

God wants us to stand up for what is good in the world. God wants us to fight for what is right. God wants us to be courageous.

SOMETHING SPECIAL

Read either of these books to the children:
David and Goliath by Mary Auld
David and Goliath by Beatrice Schenk de Regniers

DISCUSSION

Use *The Life Application Bible* and *The New Adventure Bible* commentaries to guide your discussion with the children. Ask the children why David was able to defeat a nine-foot-tall giant. (*David had faith in God to give him courage and help him fight Goliath.*) Discuss how successfully doing scary or difficult things in our lives gives us confidence to face challenging situations.

Read over 1 Samuel 17:33-37 where David tells Saul that because he has conquered other challenges, he has the faith and courage to conquer Goliath. Ask the children to share how they have successfully conquered their fears. Ask the children what challenges they would like to conquer in their lives. Help them see that God will guide them in these conquests.

Discuss the fact that God wants us to defend ourselves against bad and evil things in the world. How can we do this? Should we do what David did, or should we try to find other ways to resolve differences? What other ways?

Tell the children that, in this story, David represents goodness, and Goliath represents evil. God wants us to get rid of all of the evil things in our world. How can we keep evil things out of our lives? Be sure to share how you have conquered your fears. Tell the children about some of the challenges you faced as a child and as an adult.

SONG

"David Was a Brave Young Boy" (*"Mary Had a Little Lamb"*)

David took a bag of stones, a bag of stones, a bag of stones;
David took a bag of stones and went to find Goliath.

Goliath looked and laughed at David, laughed at David,
  laughed at David;
Goliath looked and laughed at David, but David had a plan.

David took a stone and aimed, a stone and aimed, a stone and aimed;
David took a stone and aimed, and shot it at Goliath.

That big stone hit Goliath's head, Goliath's head, Goliath's head;
That big stone hit Goliath's head, and he fell down quite dead!

David was a brave young boy, a brave young boy,
  a brave young boy;
David was a brave young boy; he was very brave!

GAME: LET'S SLAY GOLIATH

Instructions are on page 14.

CRAFT: STONES OF STRENGTH

Instructions are on page 15.

BULLETIN BOARD: OH, LORD, GIVE US STRENGTH

Instructions are on page 16.

✝ WORSHIP TIE-IN: SO BIG!

Make a large Goliath giant (see p. 13). Set it near the altar in your sanctuary. The congregation is guaranteed to be very curious about this. Invite the kids to come to the altar. Tell them the story of David and Goliath. Let the kids take turns using a baseball bat or a stick to try and break open Goliath's head. Once Goliath's head is broken open, make sure each child gets an equal amount of prizes and candy. Talk to them about how good often comes from something bad. Remind them that "of course we don't bash open someone's head when we disagree with them." Ask the children to think of ways we can resolve disagreements with one another. Help them realize that disagreements can lead us to new understandings. Tell them that God does want us to defend ourselves and work for what is right in the world. How can we do that?

GAME: LET'S SLAY GOLIATH

MATERIALS
Large white butcher paper
Colored markers
Slingshot and stones
Laminating machine and film or clear contact paper
Small round, colored sticker dots

PREPARATION
- Draw and color a large, tall picture of Goliath on the white paper.
- Laminate it.
- Hang it on the wall.

DIRECTIONS
- Let the kids use the slingshot and stones to try and hit Goliath on the forehead.
- Put a small, round sticker dot on each place that the stone hits Goliath.

PREPARATION

- Cut each wallpaper sample so it measures approximately 8" x 12".
- Fold the wallpaper sample from the bottom up, leaving about 2 inches of space at the top. Fold the top over, so it makes a flap.
- Fold each side back by approximately 1 inch. Open the sides again, and trim off the top squares. This will allow the flap to open and close. Fold the flaps back again.
- Punch three holes along each side. Punch five holes along the bottom.

DIRECTIONS

- Give each child a pouch and the strand of leather. Let the children lace the leather through the holes. Be sure not to pull the strand of leather all the way through. You need to have enough so that you can tie the ends together at the top.
- Give each child a copy of the Bible verse. Have the children slip the verse over one of the ends of the leather strand. Tie the leather strands together at the top. This allows the children to wear the pouch over their shoulders.
- Give each child two strands of yarn and have them string it through the two bottom corner holes on the pouch, then tie the yarn in a knot. Attach the beads to the ends of the yarn and tie knots in the ends, so the beads will not slip off.
- Let the children use crayons to decorate their pouches.
- Give each child five stones to carry in their pouches. Help the children remember that each stone can remind us of something good we can do in the world. Let the children decide which good things their stones can represent.

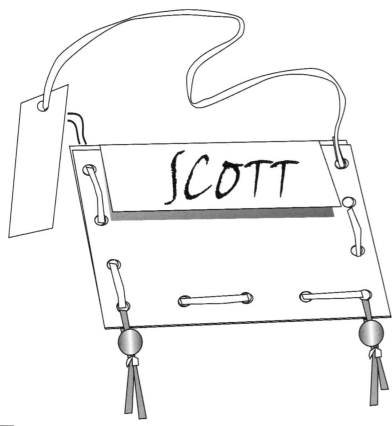

CRAFT: STONES OF STRENGTH

MATERIALS

Five colored stones per child
One 12-inch piece of leather string per child
Two 6-inch strands of yarn per child
Book of wallpaper samples
Scissors
Paper punch
Four medium-sized wooden beads with holes per child
One small laminated copy of the key Bible verse per child (see p. 13)

BULLETIN BOARD: OH, LORD, GIVE US STRENGTH

MATERIALS

Light blue paper
Bright yellow paper
Letter stencils (use die-cutting machine if available)
Gray and brown paper
Black markers
Pushpins
Scissors

PREPARATION

- Cover the board with blue paper.
- Cut out rocks from the brown and gray paper.
- Cut out the title from yellow paper and attach it to the board.

DIRECTIONS

- Give each child a brown or gray rock and a black marker.
- Tell each child to write something good they can do in the world.
- Attach the rocks to the board.

BULLETIN BOARD ILLUSTRATION

BONUS PUZZLE: WHAT'S THE MESSAGE?

Use a yellow marker to draw a line through each of these words when you find them in the puzzle. When you are finished you will have some words left over. Print the message here.

___ ___   ___ ___ ___   ___ ___ ___ ___   ___ ___ ___ ___ ___   ___ ___

___ ___ ___ ___   ___ ___ ___.

David
Hit
Am
Stones
Aim
Brave
Goliath
Sheep
Ha
Too

Bag
God
Shepherd
Helmet
Giant
Slingshot
Love
Frightened
Me
Boy

D	S	H	E	P	H	E	R	D	T
A	G	O	G	O	D	A	H	G	O
V	S	H	E	E	P	N	I	I	O
I	B	O	Y	B	A	D	T	A	G
D	T	H	E	A	M	E	L	N	O
S	L	I	N	G	S	H	O	T	L
A	I	M	L	O	R	D	V	B	I
H	E	L	M	E	T	H	E	E	A
W	I	T	H	B	R	A	V	E	T
S	T	O	N	E	S	Y	O	U	H
F	R	I	G	H	T	E	N	E	D

BONUS PUZZLE SOLUTION: WHAT'S THE MESSAGE?

Use a yellow marker to draw a line through each of these words when you find them in the puzzle. When you are finished you will have some words left over. Print the message here.

_GO_ _AND_ _THE_ _LORD_ _BE_ _WITH_ _YOU_.

David   Bag

Hit   God

Am   Shepherd

Stones   Helmet

Aim   Giant

Brave   Slingshot

Goliath   Love

Sheep   Frightened

Ha   Me

Too   Boy

D	S	H	E	P	H	E	R	D	T
A	G	O	G	O	D	A	H	G	O
Y	S	H	E	E	P	N	I	I	O
B	O	Y	B	A	D	T	A	G	
D	T	H	E	A	M	E	L	N	O
S	L	I	N	G	S	H	O	T	L
A	I	M	L	O	R	D	V	B	I
H	E	L	M	E	T	H	E	E	A
W	I	T	H	B	R	A	V	E	T
S	T	O	N	E	S	Y	O	U	H
F	R	I	G	H	T	E	N	E	D

THE PEACEABLE KINGDOM

Offer this program at any time of the year. See if you can have a petting zoo visit your children. Set up an area with green outdoor patio carpet, large boulders, and tree stumps. Use a large blue tarp to make a small lake to add to the scene.

 ## SCRIPTURE: ISAIAH 11:6-9 (NIV)

Key Verse (Isaiah 11:9): "They will neither harm nor destroy
   on all my holy mountain,
for the earth will be full of the knowledge of the LORD
   as the waters cover the sea."

 ## THEME

God wants all people to get along with each other. In this story God has animals who are natural enemies live together peacefully. God wants people to get along peacefully also.

 ## SOMETHING SPECIAL

Read this story to the children:
The Peaceable Kingdom by Ewa Zadrzynska
Have one puppet or stuffed animal for each animal in the story. Give each child a puppet or animal to hold, and tell the children to stand off to the side of the room. As you read the story, the child holding that puppet or animal will come to the center of the room and do what the story says to do. At the end of the story, have the children sit on the floor together holding their animals/puppets. Take a photo of your "Peaceable Kingdom." Post this photo on your church website.

 ## DISCUSSION

Talk about the wars, the violence, and the cruelty we have in our world today. Is this good or bad? Why? Ask the children if they have experienced cruelty or violence.

What does it feel like when someone does something to hurt you? Why do you think people do things that are cruel and violent? Does God want us to be cruel to one another?

How do you think God views violence and war? How can we live our lives so we are peaceful? How can we show kindness to others?

Adapt your discussion to the ages you are working with as well as to the current world situation. Always assure children that God is watching out for them and that the adults in their world are doing everything they can to make the world a safe place.

 ## ART EXPERIENCE

Check your local library and find a book that has a copy of the painting "The Peaceable Kingdom" by Edward Hicks. Show the children a copy of the painting. Explain that Edward Hicks was a minister who lived from 1780 to 1830. He enjoyed this scripture, and he too wanted a world that was peaceful and free from violence. So he created a painting called "The Peaceable Kingdom," based on this story. He liked this painting so much that he painted more than fifty additional "Peaceable Kingdoms." They are all just a bit different, and many of them are in museums around the world. See if you can find several different paintings that Edward Hicks did of this story, and show them to the children. Let the children compare the similarities and differences in the paintings you view.

 ## SONG

"God Wants Us to Live in Peace" *("If You're Happy")*

Oh, the wolf came to live with the lamb.
Oh, the wolf came to live with the lamb.
Oh, the wolf came to live; oh, the wolf came to live;
Oh, the wolf came to live with the lamb.

Oh, the leopard laid down with the goat.
Oh, the leopard laid down with the goat.
Oh, the leopard laid down; oh, the leopard laid down;
Oh, the leopard laid down with the goat.

Oh, the cow and the bear ate together.
Oh, the cow and the bear ate together.
Oh, the cow and the bear; oh, the cow and the bear;
Oh, the cow and the bear ate together.

Oh, the lion and the ox shared the straw.
Oh, the lion and the ox shared the straw.
Oh, the lion and the ox; oh, the lion and the ox;
Oh, the lion and the ox shared the straw.

God wants us to love and live in peace.
God wants us to love and live in peace.
God wants us to love; God wants us to love;
God wants us to love and live in peace.

ACTIVITY IDEA

Let the kids sing and act out this song with the puppets and stuffed animals.

CRAFT: MY PEACEABLE KINGDOM

Instructions are on pages 20-21.

GAME: PUT THE PEACEABLE KINGDOM BACK TOGETHER

Instructions are on page 21.

SCIENCE EXPERIENCE

Bring in a short, well-illustrated book about each animal depicted in this story. Let each child (or group of children) choose an animal to learn about. Let each child (or group) tell about the chosen animal.

BULLETIN BOARD: (CHURCH NAME)'S PEACEABLE KINGDOM

Instructions are on page 21.

WORSHIP TIE-IN: LIVING IN PEACE

Plan a congregational worship service that revolves around living peacefully with those who have different ethnic, racial, and religious backgrounds. Invite the children to present the story of "The Peaceable Kingdom" for congregational worship. Let them act out the story and sing the song with the puppets and animals as you did during your class.

CRAFT: MY PEACEABLE KINGDOM

MATERIALS
One colored sticker of each animal in this story per child
One large sheet of green cardstock paper (at least 11" x 17") per child
One large sheet of white cardboard (at least 11" x 17") per child
One glue stick per child
Laminating machine and film or clear contact paper
One resealable plastic bag per child
One 6-inch strand of white yarn per child
One typed copy of the story per child
Book tape

PREPARATION

- Place one sticker of each animal into each plastic bag. Each child will have a bag of animal stickers.
- Laminate and cut out one copy of the story for each child.

DIRECTIONS

- Give each child a piece of green paper, a piece of cardboard, and a glue stick. Have the children glue the green paper to the cardboard.
- Give each child a bag of animals. Tell them to stick the animals to the green paper so they tell the story of "The Peaceable Kingdom."
- Use tape to attach a yarn loop to the back of each child's "Peaceable Kingdom."
- Glue a copy of the story to the back of the picture.

GAME: PUT THE PEACEABLE KINGDOM BACK TOGETHER

DIRECTIONS

Set up a re-creation of The Peaceable Kingdom using stuffed animals or beanbag animals. Have all the children (except for one) cover their eyes. The child whose eyes are uncovered will remove an animal and put it behind his or her back. The first child to discover which animal is missing and properly replace it, gets to remove and hide the next animal. Keep playing until each child has had a turn.

BULLETIN BOARD: (CHURCH NAME)'S PEACEABLE KINGDOM

MATERIALS

Blue, green, brown, orange, and bright yellow fadeless paper
White and gray paper
White batting
Large drawings of animals (coloring books or flannel board pattern books)
Crayons
Glue
Pushpins
Letter stencils (use die-cutting machine if available)
Scissors

DIRECTIONS

- Cover the top half of the board with blue fadeless paper.
- Cut the green paper to look like hills and use it to cover the bottom half of the board.
- Cut a tree out of brown paper. Cut leaves from the green paper. Attach the tree and leaves to the board.
- Cut rocks out of the gray paper and attach them to the board.
- Cut the title "(Church)'s Peaceable Kingdom" out of orange paper and attach it to the board.
- Cut the sun out of yellow paper and attach it to the board.
- Cut clouds out of white paper. Glue white batting to the clouds. Attach the clouds to the board.
- Give each child an animal picture to color. Cut out each picture, attach it to the board, and create your very own "Peaceable Kingdom" picture.

BULLETIN BOARD ILLUSTRATION

OUR CHURCH'S PEACEABLE KINGDOM

BONUS PUZZLE: GOD'S PEACEABLE KINGDOM

Can you decipher this puzzle (based on Isaiah 11:6-9 NIV)?

The 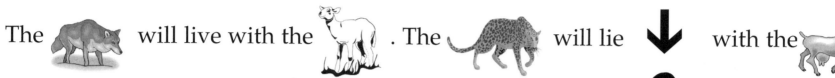 will live with the . The will lie with the .

The and the and the 2gether. And a little will lead them.

The will feed with the . Their young will lie 2gether.

And the 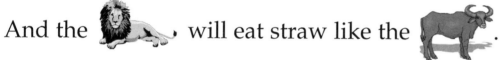 will eat straw like the .

The will play near the hole of the .

And the young will put his into the 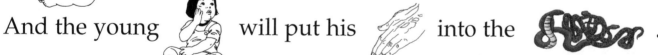.

They will neither h + nor destroy on all my holy  4 the will be full

of the knowledge of the LORD as the ~~~~~ cover the C.

BONUS PUZZLE SOLUTION: GOD'S PEACEABLE KINGDOM

Can you decipher this puzzle (based on Isaiah 11:6-9 NIV)?

The **wolf** will live with the **lamb**. The **leopard** will lie **down** with the **goat**.

The **calf** and the **lion** and the **yearling** 2gether. And a little **child** will lead them.

The **cow** will feed with the **bear**. Their young will lie **down** 2gether.

And the **lion** will eat straw like the **ox** .

The **infant** will play near the hole of the **cobra**.

And the young **child** will put his **hand** into the **viper's nest** .

They will neither h + **arm** nor destroy on all my holy **mountain**. 4 the **earth** will be

full of the knowledge of the LORD as the **waters** cover the C.

A KID FOR A KING (KING JOSIAH)

Offer this program at any time of the year. Set up the room to look like a king's court. Find a large chair, and make it into a throne by covering it with an attractive slipcover. Place a crown, a scepter, and an attractive robe on the throne. Put a length of red carpet leading up to the throne. Purchase some inexpensive plaster figurines and place them around the room. Make a scroll of the Ten Commandments and have it sitting nearby but out of sight. You'll need two empty paper towel cardboard rolls, ten sheets of paper, large markers, laminating machine and film or clear contact paper, a twelve-inch leather shoelace and clear book tape. Print one commandment on each sheet of paper. Laminate the ten sheets. Tape them together on both sides, making sure they are in the correct order. Tape the commandments to the paper towel rolls to make a scroll. Tie it together with the leather shoelace. Also have several Bibles hidden in the room.

SCRIPTURE: 2 KINGS 22–23; 2 CHRONICLES 34–35

Key Verse (2 Kings 22:2): "He did what was right in the sight of the LORD, and walked in all the way of his father David; he did not turn aside to the right or to the left."

THEME

It's important to study and become familiar with the word of God so that we can be obedient to God's laws.

SOMETHING SPECIAL

Tell a simplified version of this Bible story in your own words.

DISCUSSION

How do you think it would be to become a king at the age of eight? You would be in charge! Do you think it would be a good thing or a bad thing for an eight-year-old to be in charge? Why?

How do you think Josiah felt when he learned that he was the king? Do you think he was scared, excited, or happy?

Discuss the changes that Josiah made. The people had been disobeying God and God's commandments. They were worshiping idols rather than worshiping God. Is it good or bad to worship idols? Is it good or bad to worship God? Why or why not?

What happens when people refuse to obey the word of God? What happens when we obey the word of God?

ACTIVITY: SMASHING IDOLS

Instructions are on page 25.

SONG

"King Josiah" (*"London Bridge"*)
King Josiah was eight years old, eight years old, eight years old.
King Josiah was eight years old when he began to rule.

King Josiah was very sad, very sad, very sad.
King Josiah was very sad with what the people did.

King Josiah broke the idols, broke the idols, broke the idols.
King Josiah broke the idols and said, "Let's follow God."

King Josiah taught his people, taught his people, taught his people.
King Josiah taught his people to follow all God's rules.

GAME: FIND IT!

Instructions are on page 25.

 CRAFT: ROYAL CROWNS

Instructions are on page 26.

 BULLETIN BOARD: A WISE KING

Instructions are on page 27.

 WORSHIP TIE-IN: WHOM SHOULD WE WORSHIP?

Invite the children to sit by the altar with you. Talk a little about King Josiah and how his people were worshiping idols. Have a stuffed animal with you. Tell the children that this animal is your idol.

"I worship this animal. When I want to do well at work, I grab hold of his tail and pray to him to help me do well at work. When I want it to be a nice day, I grab hold of his ears and pray to him for a nice day."

Soon, the children are going to tell you that you shouldn't worship this animal. Say, "Well, why shouldn't I worship this animal. I really like it. It's my favorite stuffed animal, so I want to worship it."

When the children again tell you no, say, "Well, then, whom should I worship?" *(God, and only God.)*

"Why should I worship God?" *(Because God is the one who can help, not that animal. Besides God tells us to worship only God.)*

Explain that the people in this story were worshiping idols rather than worshiping God. That made God very upset. King Josiah told everyone that we have to worship God and only God. It is God who created us. It is God who loves us and wants to help us. These idols have no power. They cannot do anything to help us.

 ACTIVITY: SMASHING IDOLS

MATERIALS

Inexpensive plaster figures   Gold spray paint
Sheets of plastic and newspaper

PREPARATION
- Place the figurines on newspaper and spray with gold spray paint. Let them dry.
- Cover the floor with plastic.

DIRECTIONS
- Talk about false idols with the children.
- Tell the children that some people came into our classroom and left all of these false idols behind. What do you think of that? What should we do about that?
- Let the kids take turns smashing the false idols on the plastic. *(A note of caution: be careful with plaster as it tends to fly apart and can make jagged edges.)*

 GAME: FIND IT!

MATERIALS

A scroll (see p. 24) and several Bibles

PREPARATION
- Hide the scroll and Bibles in the room.

DIRECTIONS
- Give hints that some things "seem to be missing from the room."
- Let the kids see if they can find the missing items without knowing what they are looking for.
- Act surprised, just like King Josiah did in the story.
- Talk about what we should do with these items.

CRAFT: ROYAL CROWNS

MATERIALS

One 24" x 6" piece of gold cardboard per child
Self-stick Velcro
Glitter glue and regular glue
Colorful stones and sequins
Newspaper

PREPARATION

- Cut each piece of gold cardboard into a crown shape.
- Place the sequins and colored stones into separate containers.
- Type up a copy of the Bible verse for each child. Laminate these.

DIRECTIONS

- Measure each crown to each child's head. Stick Velcro to each crown so the crown can be snugly attached to each child's head.
- Give each child a crown to decorate with glitter glue, sequins, and colored stones. Have the children attach the Bible verse to their crowns.
- Let the crowns dry flat overnight before wearing them. Let kids carry them home flat on a folded sheet of newspaper.

CROWN PATTERN
(Adjust size as needed)

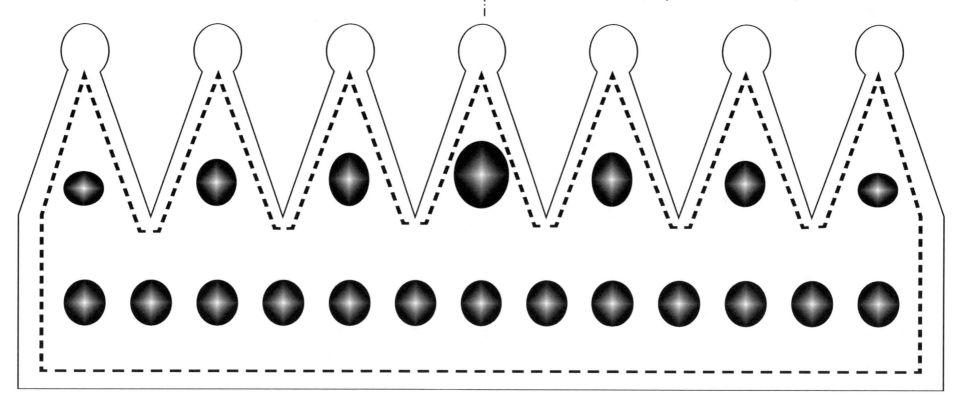

BULLETIN BOARD: A WISE KING

MATERIALS

Shiny blue wrapping paper
Shiny gold wrapping paper
White cardstock paper
Pushpins
Gel pens
Glue
Glitter glue
Sequins
Scissors
Letter stencils (use die-cutting machine if available)

PREPARATION

- Cover the board with the shiny blue paper.
- Cut a crown out of the shiny gold paper. Decorate it with glitter glue and sequins. Let it dry.
- Attach the crown to the board.
- Cut the title out of the shiny gold paper. Attach it to the board.
- Cut interesting shapes out of the white cardstock paper.

DIRECTIONS

- Give each child a white shape and a glitter pen.
- Tell the children to write things that we can do that will please God on their white shape.
- Attach the white shapes to the board.

BULLETIN BOARD ILLUSTRATION

BONUS PUZZLE: KING JOSIAH WORD FINDER

Use a yellow marker or crayon to draw a line through each word you find. When you are finished, you will discover a special message. Write it here. (Hint: Make sure the clue "I" isn't part of another word.)

___ ___ ___ ___ ___ ___ ___ ___ ___ ___ ___ ___ ___ ___

Passover	Judah	Priest
Book	Sad	Me
Love	Temple	Repair
Robe	Angry	Eight
Burned	Humbled	Rule
Money	Obey	Idols
I	Covenant	To
Heart	Awe	Help
Law	Father	At
Hilkiah	Ruled	Go
Lord	Jerusalem	God

R	M	E	J	U	D	A	H	H	E	L	P	B
E	H	R	U	L	E	D	♛	B	O	O	K	U
P	E	♛	P	R	I	E	S	T	A	W	E	R
A	A	T	E	M	P	L	E	R	U	L	E	N
I	R	♛	J	O	S	I	A	H	♛	I	E	E
R	T	H	I	L	K	I	A	H	W	D	I	D
♛	H	T	O	♛	L	O	R	D	A	O	G	♛
M	U	O	B	L	A	S	A	D	S	L	H	F
O	M	A	E	O	W	G	O	D	♛	S	T	A
N	B	A	Y	V	G	O	O	D	♛	K	♛	T
E	L	T	♛	E	A	N	G	R	Y	I	R	H
Y	E	P	A	S	S	O	V	E	R	N	O	E
G	D	C	O	V	E	N	A	N	T	G	B	R
O	I	J	E	R	U	S	A	L	E	M	E	♛

BONUS PUZZLE SOLUTION: KING JOSIAH WORD FINDER

Use a yellow marker or crayon to draw a line through each word you find. When you are finished, you will discover a special message. Write it here.

JOSIAH WAS A GOOD KING

Passover	Judah	Priest
Book	Sad	Me
Love	Temple	Repair
Robe	Angry	Eight
Burned	Humbled	Rule
Money	Obey	Idols
I	Covenant	To
Heart	Awe	Help
Law	Father	At
Hilkiah	Ruled	Go
Lord	Jerusalem	God

R	M	E	J	U	D	A	H	H	E	L	P	B
E	H	R	U	L	E	D	👑	B	O	O	K	U
P	E	👑	P	R	I	E	S	T	A	W	E	R
A	A	T	E	M	P	L	E	R	U	L	E	N
I	R	👑	J	O	S	I	A	H	👑	I	E	E
R	T	H	I	L	K	I	A	H	W	D	I	D
👑	H	T	O	👑	L	O	R	D	A	O	G	👑
M	U	O	B	L	A	S	A	D	S	L	H	F
O	M	A	E	O	W	G	O	D	👑	S	T	A
N	B	A	Y	V	G	O	O	D	👑	K	👑	T
E	L	T	👑	E	A	N	G	R	Y	I	R	H
Y	E	P	A	S	S	O	V	E	R	N	O	E
G	D	C	O	V	E	N	A	N	T	G	B	R
O	+	J	E	R	U	S	A	L	E	M	E	👑

DANIEL IN THE LIONS' DEN

Offer this program at any time of the year. Set up the room to look like a dungeon (lions' den). Make grated coverings to attach to the windows, have some boulders strewn about the room. Move the chairs and tables out, so the children will have to sit on the floor or on the boulders. Position stuffed lions about the room. Have a large, lighted Christmas angel sitting in the room.

SCRIPTURE: DANIEL 6

Key Verses (Daniel 6:26-27):
"For he is the living God,
  enduring forever.
His kingdom shall never be destroyed,
  and his dominion has no end.
He delivers and rescues,
  he works signs and wonders in heaven and on earth;
for he has saved Daniel
  from the power of the lions."

THEME

God watches over us and protects us, if we put our trust in him.

SOMETHING SPECIAL

Read any of these books to the children:
  Daniel in the Lions' Den by Mary Auld
  Daniel and the Lions' Den by Christine L. Benagh
  The Story of Daniel in the Lions' Den by Michael McCarthy

SONG

"Oh Daniel!" (*"If You're Happy"*)
Have all but three of the children sing the song. Those three children will shout out the words in parentheses.

Oh, Daniel prayed to God three times a day! (*Good job!*)
Oh, Daniel prayed to God three times a day! (*Good job!*)
Oh, Daniel prayed to God; oh Daniel prayed to God;
Oh, Daniel prayed to God three times a day! (*Good job!*)

Oh, Daniel wouldn't pray to the king! (*Right on!*)
Oh, Daniel wouldn't pray to the king! (*Right on!*)
Oh, Daniel wouldn't pray; oh Daniel wouldn't pray;
Oh, Daniel wouldn't pray to the king! (*Right on!*)

Oh, Daniel was tossed to the lions! (*Oh, no!*)
Oh, Daniel was tossed to the lions! (*Oh, no!*)
Oh, Daniel was tossed; oh, Daniel was tossed;
Oh, Daniel was tossed to the lions! (*Oh, no!*)

Oh, the angel came and shut the lions' mouths! (*All right!*)
Oh, the angel came and shut the lions' mouths! (*All right!*)
Oh, the angel came along; oh, the angel came along;
Oh, the angel came and shut the lions' mouths! (*All right!*)

Oh, the lions didn't gobble Daniel up! (*I'm glad!*)
Oh, the lions didn't gobble Daniel up! (*I'm glad!*)
Oh, the lions didn't gobble; oh, the lions didn't gobble;
Oh, the lions didn't gobble Daniel up! (*I'm glad!*)

Oh, Daniel obeyed the Lord! (*Yeah, Daniel!*)
Oh, Daniel obeyed the Lord! (*Yeah, Daniel!*)
Oh, Daniel obeyed; oh, Daniel obeyed;
Oh, Daniel obeyed the Lord! (*Yeah, Daniel!*)

GAME: LION BOWLING

Instructions are on page 31.

CRAFT: DANIEL, LION, AND ANGEL PUPPETS

Instructions are on page 31.

ACTIVITY: DANIEL IN THE LIONS' DEN

Let the children help tell the story using the flannel board pieces.

BULLETIN BOARD: LOOK WHO'S IN THE LIONS' DEN

Instructions are on page 33.

WORSHIP TIE-IN: BRAVE DANIEL

Let the kids use their puppets to present a puppet show of "Daniel in the Lions' Den" for congregational worship. Let them sing the song, "Oh, Daniel."

GAME: LION BOWLING

MATERIALS

Ten empty, clean, full-sized Pringles chips cans
Clear book tape
Ten lions
Scissors
One tennis ball
Masking tape
Yellow contact paper
Laminating machine and film or clear contact paper
Small prizes for winners
Golden yellow cardstock paper

PREPARATION

• Cover each can with yellow contact paper. Weight the cans with anything heavy (rocks, clay). All cans should be the same weight. Tape the lids to the cans.

• Make ten yellow copies of the lion pattern on page 32.
• Laminate the lion patterns. Cut out the lions.
• Tape one lion to each Pringles can.
• Set up the lions the same way you would set up bowling pins.
• Use masking tape to mark off the bowling lane.

DIRECTIONS

• Let each child take a turn at "Lion Bowling." Scoring is one point for each pin knocked down. The child with the highest score can be given a small prize.

CRAFT: DANIEL, LION, AND ANGEL PUPPETS

MATERIALS

Three paint stirring sticks per child
One Daniel pattern, one lion pattern, and one angel pattern per child
Twelve strips of brown paper per child
One copy of the key verses per child (p. 30)
White glue
Gold and silver glitter glue
Crayons

PREPARATION

• Copy and cut the patterns (p. 32).
• Type up, print, and cut out copies of the key verses.

DIRECTIONS

• Give each child a lion pattern, a Daniel pattern, and an angel pattern to color.
• Give each child the twelve paper strips. Show them how to wind the strips around their fingers to make paper curls. Have the children glue the paper curls to the lions' faces.
• Give three paint stirring sticks to each child.
• Have the children glue the lion, Daniel, and angel puppets to the paint sticks.
• Give each child a copy of the key verses, and tell them to glue it to their Daniel puppet.

PUPPET PATTERNS
LION PATTERN

Adjust size
as needed

DANIEL PATTERN

ANGEL PATTERN

32

BULLETIN BOARD: LOOK WHO'S IN THE LION'S DEN

MATERIALS

Gray, white, tan, brown, black, dark blue construction or cardstock paper

Daniel, angel, and lion patterns (p. 32)

Scissors, crayons, markers, glue

Pushpins

Letter stencils (use die-cutting machine if available)

PREPARATION AND DIRECTIONS

- Cover the bottom half of the bulletin board with black paper. Cover the top half of the board with gray paper. Cut a window out of the white paper and use a black marker to make bars on the window. Attach the window to the top of the den.

- Use letter stencils or the die-cutting machine to cut out the title from the dark blue paper. Attach title to the board.
- Enlarge and copy pattern of Daniel and the angel.
- Enlarge and make 6 copies of the lion pattern.
- Cut stones out of the brown paper, and attach them to the board, so it looks like there are rocks in the den.
- Attach Daniel, the lions, and the angel to the board.
- Make a copy of the key verses. Make it into a sign and place it so it looks like Daniel is holding it.

BULLETIN BOARD ILLUSTRATION

BONUS PUZZLE: WHO WATCHED OVER DANIEL?

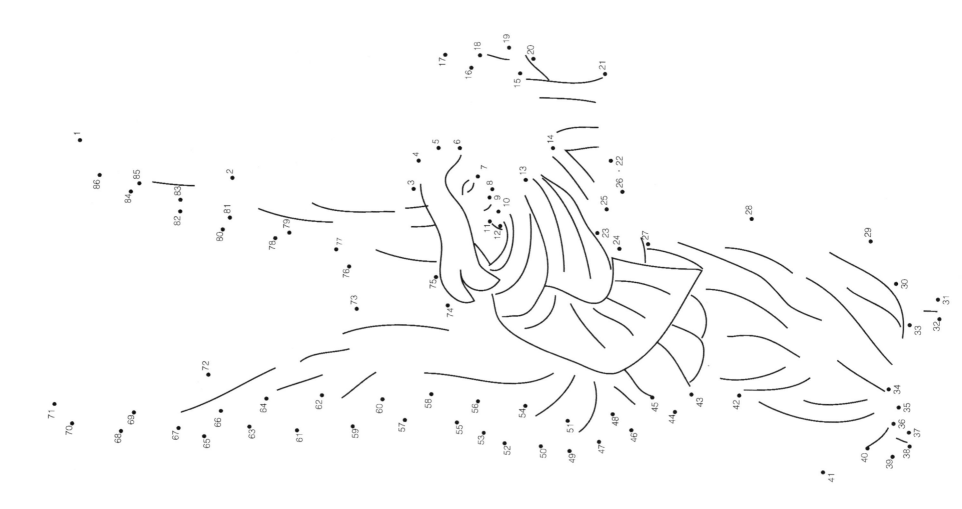

BONUS PUZZLE SOLUTION: WHO WATCHED OVER DANIEL?

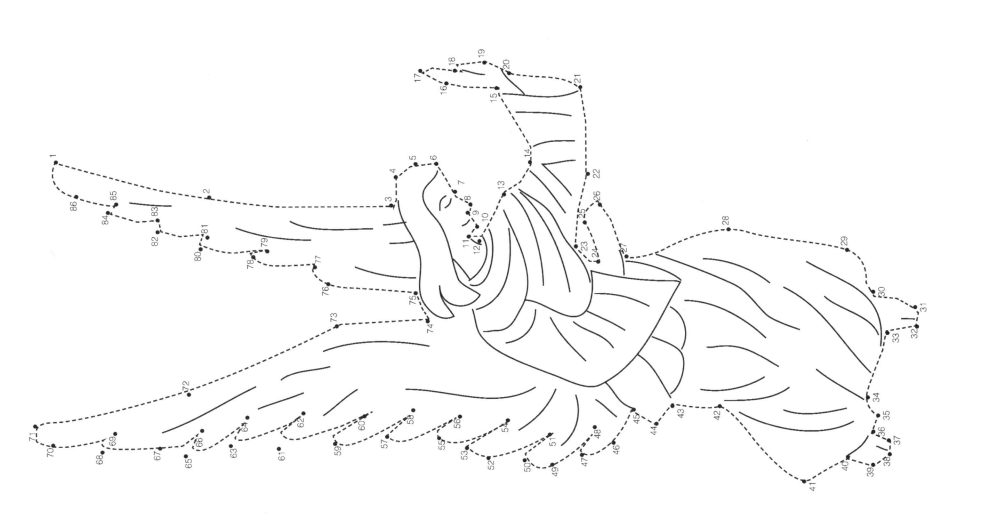

AMAZING ADVENTURES

SONSATIONAL SUNDAY CELEBRATION

It's time for a *Sonsational* Sunday Celebration! You've spent several weeks meeting some remarkable people who've had some Amazing Adventures. Focus this program on reliving all of the excitement you've shared together as you've become acquainted with some awesome people.

Use your fellowship hall or another large area for this program. Adapt this program to fit your space. If you do not have a large room to accommodate this program, you can use one room for the Gathering Place and a different Sunday school room for each Adventure Stop.

Combine all children—kindergarten through grade five—and have some Amazing Adventures with all ages participating together. Invite parents to participate with their children. This allows parents the opportunity to learn about what their children have studied in these lessons. It opens the door for parent-child faith-based discussions and allows families the opportunity to participate as a family unit. It's always interesting to see the similarities and differences in the discussions from each age group.

For this program, the children and their parents will travel to a variety of Adventure Stops, where everyone will have the opportunity to visit with each of your new Bible friends. You can once again share some Amazing Adventures with them. The six Adventure Stops include: The Construction Site (Tower of Babel), The Bulrushes (Baby in a Basket/Moses), The Battlefield (One Big Giant/David and Goliath), The Meadow (Peaceable Kingdom), The Royal Palace (A Kid for a King/King Josiah), and The Lions' Den (Daniel and the Lion's Den).

Set these up ahead of time in six different locations around the room or in different rooms. Set up a Gathering Place in the middle of the room where everyone will gather to begin your Amazing Adventures. If necessary, select a separate room for the Gathering Place. Put a large area rug in the middle, so children have a place to sit. Set up chairs for the parents around the perimeter of the rug. Create large, colorful, eye-catching signs for each Amazing Adventure Stop.

Make a passport for each child. You'll need an 8½" x 5½" piece of white cardstock per child. Fold it in half. Decorate it to look like a passport. As children enter the fellowship hall, take an instant photo of each child and glue it to the front of their passport. Have the children sign their passports with thin-tipped blue marker. See sample on page 40. Hold on to the passports until it's time to begin traveling. The children can be given their passports while they are still in the Gathering Place.

Purchase one rubber stamp that highlights each of the Old Testament stories you have shared. You'll need six stamp pads in six different colors. Put the appropriate stamp and a stamp pad at each Adventure Stop. As the children visit each stop, they can add a stamp to their passports. Passports should be stamped on the **inside.** The back of the passport will be used at one of the Adventure Stops, so it needs to be kept free of stamps.

You'll need at least two teachers to set up and host each Adventure Stop. Let the families visit the Adventure Stops in any order they choose. Families must travel as a family unit. The teachers at each location should review the Bible stories and characters in each story with the children. While at each Adventure Stop, the children and their parents will participate in each activity offered. Parents are required to participate rather than just observe.

Ask the members of the congregation who helped with each story to reprise their roles for this program.

Let parents and children know that this is a "casual and comfy" dress event. Dress to play and be messy! Another idea is to let parents and children don Bible costumes (page xii).

See pages 37-39 for each Amazing Adventure Stop instructions and the materials you need at each stop.

Begin the program in the Gathering Place with kids on the rug and parents in the chairs. Have a brief program where you welcome the children and their parents; have a time of prayer and music and explain what everyone will do.

 ## SCRIPTURE: ISAIAH 41:10

Key Verse: "Do not fear, for I am with you,
   do not be afraid, for I am your God;
I will strengthen you, I will help you,
   I will uphold you with my victorious right hand."

THEME

God leads us on some Amazing Adventures through life. These adventures can be scary, exciting, and even fun. As we go through each of these Amazing Adventures, we have the opportunity to grow in our faith and become strong people of God. God wants us to be strong and to do the Lord's work in the world. God wants us to remember that we are loved, and God wants us to share this love with everyone. God wants us to set good examples in all that we do. God wants us to live in peace and harmony with one another. In each of these six stories, God has been there to give courage and help to people.

STORY: THE PEACEABLE KINGDOM

Have a group of children act out this story as you read it aloud. See page 19.

DISCUSSION

Talk once again with the children and now with their parents about how God had animals who are natural enemies come together in peace and harmony. How can we as people learn to live in peace and harmony?

SONG

"God Wants Us to Live in Peace" (See p. 19). Make this into slides, using PowerPoint or other presentation software, and project the words onto a large screen so everyone can sing it together.

TRAVELIN' TIME

Explain that each family will travel to a different Amazing Adventure, where they will participate in the activity as a family. Have each child stamp the *inside* of their passport when they arrive at each Adventure Stop. The back of the passport will be used for something at one of the Adventure Stops, so it needs to be free of stamps. Parents are expected to participate (rather than observe) in all activities with their children.

STATION 1: THE TOWER OF BABEL

Provide a variety of blocks (wooden, Lego, Duplo) and tables for "tower building." Have kids stamp the *inside* of their passports.

Ask several members of the congregation to help you by saying the Lord's Prayer in a different language. Remind everyone that even though we find it difficult to hear and understand everyone, God does this with ease all the time!

Remind the children that we used a variety of methods to build our towers. One group built a tower without speaking. How did they communicate? Another built the tower while speaking English. There was another group where everyone spoke a different language. How did this group communicate?

Let each family experience a different way of building a tower (without speaking, while speaking English, and with each person speaking a different language).

See what kind of unique towers each family can build. Take digital photos of families building towers. Post these on your church website.

STATION 2: THE BABY IN A BASKET

You'll need blue, several shades of green, brown and beige tempera paints, paint brushes, small sponge squares, a large piece of white butcher paper, a long table, pie tins, and clear book tape. Prior to the program, have someone paint a scene of baby Moses floating on the river with

Miriam standing on the river bank. Have Moses' mother off to the side. DO NOT paint in the bulrushes. Let this dry for at least 24 hours before the program.

Have the kids stamp the *inside* of their passports when they arrive.

Pour several shades of the green tempera paints into pie tins. Lay the picture on the table. Let the kids and parents take turns sponge painting the green bulrushes onto the painting. Make sure people don't paint so many bulrushes that they obliterate the painting. If you expect a large turnout, consider making several paintings of this scene. When the mural has dried thoroughly, hang it up in a prominent location for everyone to see and enjoy.

STATION 3: ONE BIG GIANT (DAVID AND GOLIATH)

Perch Goliath (p. 14) against the wall. Have a slingshot, a bucket of beanbags and some colored self-stick dots.

Remind kids to stamp the *inside* of their passports.

Let each parent and child take a turn at shooting a beanbag at Goliath. Attach a colored dot to each *hit*. Is anyone strong enough to knock Goliath over? Talk about how God gave David the courage to fight Goliath. Also discuss how God gives us courage to conquer our enemies without resorting to fighting.

STATION 4: THE PEACEABLE KINGDOM

You'll need a variety of animal masks. Purchase the animal paper plates in the grocery stores. Punch holes in each side, and attach elastic bands so the masks can be slipped on and off. Cut eye holes too. You'll also need a cassette or CD player with a recording of lively children's Christian music and a small basket for collecting the morning offering.

Have kids stamp the *inside* of their passports.

Have each group of people sit in a circle and put on an animal mask. You are going to play Hot Potato. As the music is played, the basket will be passed around the circle. When the music stops, the person holding it can drop an offering inside the basket. Keep playing until all offerings are collected. If you have people waiting for this Amazing Adventure, people can leave as soon as they have given their offering. Others can take their place in the circle.

Create a giant floor-sized puzzle of The Peaceable Kingdom. Color copy large photos of each animal in the story. You can also purchase coloring books featuring animals or use flannel board pattern books for each animal. Copy each picture onto white paper and color it. Glue pictures onto poster board to make a Peaceable Kingdom scene. Let it dry thoroughly. Cut the poster board into puzzle pieces. Let people try to put the puzzle together. If you expect a large turnout, create several puzzles.

STATION 5: A KID FOR A KING (KING JOSIAH)

You'll need six large, clean ice-cream containers (from an ice-cream store), six beanbags, six pieces of gold poster board, heavy-duty scissors, small prizes, a stapler with staples, and masking tape. From the gold poster board, cut out 6 crowns that will fit snugly around the opening of each ice-cream container. Staple the crowns around the opening of each ice-cream container, so they fit firmly without slipping down. If desired decorate the crowns with shiny stickers, stones, and sequins. Put a masking tape line on the floor. Scatter the six crowns at six different locations around your area. Drop a different set of prizes into each bucket. For example one bucket will have key rings, another bucket will have mini candy bars.

Have each child stamp the *inside* of his or her passport.

Talk about the story with each group of people. Remind everyone that King Josiah, unlike his father, was a good king who always strove to do his best.

Let each person have a turn at tossing the beanbags into the buckets. Let's follow King Josiah's example and do our best to get the beanbags into the crowns. Every time a person gets a beanbag into a bucket, he or she can take a prize out of that bucket.

STATION 6: DANiEL iN THE LiONS' DEN

Set up the Lion Bowling Game (p. 31). Have lots of lion and angel stickers.

Talk about the story with those who visit this Amazing Adventure. Talk about how the angel took care of Daniel and allowed him to defeat his fear of the lions. The angel kept Daniel safe.

Let everyone have a chance at Lion Bowling. Children can be given one sticker for each pin they knock down. The stickers go on the **back** of the passport.

CLOSING: HEY GOD!

Have everyone return to the Gathering Place. Thank the parents and children for coming to your Amazing Adventures *Sonsational* Sunday Celebration Program.

Review the Scripture memory verse and remind all of those present that God loves them, cares for them, and will always be there to help them. God always wants to give us strength, courage, and comfort. We are God's people who are deserving of God's love!

Leader: Hey God! Thanks for creating all these wonderful parents and great kids!

All: Praise the Lord! YeaaaaaAAAAYYY GOD!

Leader: Hey God! Thanks for loving us *so much!*

All: Praise the Lord! YeaaaaaAAAAYYY GOD!

Leader: Hey God! Thanks for telling us stories that help us learn stuff we need to know!

All: Praise the Lord! YeaaaaaAAAAYYY GOD!

Leader: Hey God! Thanks for bringing us together today for a time of fun learning!

All: Praise the Lord! YeaaaaaAAAAYYY GOD!

Leader: Hey God! Let us go forth now, giving thanks and praising you for all your good works. Give us courage and strength to do the right things, and help us share your love with EVERYONE!

All: Praise the Lord! YeaaaaaAAAAYYY GOD!

ILLUSTRATION OF PASSPORT

| FRONT | INSIDE | BACK |

church name

photo

name

AMAZING ADVENTURES

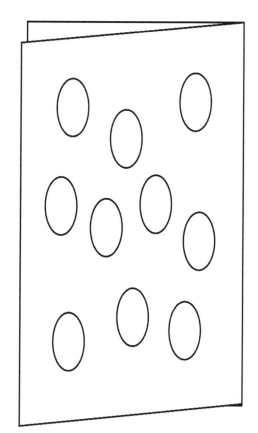

Section Two

JESUS IS COMING!

Advent is a time of preparation for the birth of Jesus. It takes place on the four Sundays preceding Christmas day. Waiting for the birth of a new baby into a family is always filled with excitement, joy, wonder, and concern. As you prepare to work with the children, pause to think of how Mary and Joseph must have felt as they waited for their beloved son, Jesus, to be born. They had been told they were to be the earthly parents of the Savior of the world. What color hair would Jesus have? What color eyes would he have? Who would he look like? What would he be like? Mary and Joseph were probably no different from any new parents awaiting the birth of a child. Did they worry about being good parents? Did they wonder if they were up to the challenge of raising God's son?

These Advent lessons will focus on learning about some of the symbols associated with Christmas. You and the children will deepen your faith as you learn about the Christmas tree, the candy cane, the Christmas wreath, and the angels. These four weeks of lessons will lead you into a joyous Christmas celebration that gives praise to God for the most magnificent of all gifts: God's son, Jesus!

On Epiphany, "The Kings Are Coming" will help you experience a *Sonsational* Sunday Celebration that will lead you on a joyous journey, where the children, their parents, and you will enjoy a time of celebrating and remembering.

WEEK 1: THE CHRISTMAS TREE

 ## SCRIPTURE: ISAIAH 11:1-3

Key Verse (Isaiah 11:1): "A shoot shall come out from the stump of Jesse, and a branch shall grow out of his roots."

 ## THEME

God's love is everlasting.

 ## SOMETHING SPECIAL

Share this story with the children:
The Legend of the Christmas Tree by Rick Osborne (There is also a shorter board book version of this story.)

Consider making this into a visual presentation, using PowerPoint or other presentational software. Have one person read the story from the book while the other person runs the presentation.

DISCUSSION

Discuss the evergreen color of the Christmas tree. It reminds us of God's everlasting love. Green reminds us of new life, which we have in Jesus. The top of the tree points to Heaven where God lives. The Bible verse speaks of the stump of a tree that is left after that tree has been chopped down. A shoot (a new tree) will grow out of that stump. That new shoot (tree) represents Jesus who will be born. He will be our Savior and bring us new life.

 ## ACTIVITY: SPONGE PAINT A CHRISTMAS TREE

Instructions are on page 43.

 ## SONG

"O, Christmas Tree"
Teach the children to sing this song (pp. 262-263 in *The Good Times Songbook* by James Leisy).

 ## CRAFT: A CHRISTMAS GIFT

Instructions are on pages 43-44.

 ## WORSHIP TIE-IN: O CHRISTMAS TREE

Place a large artificial Christmas tree on display near the altar in your sanctuary. String it with miniature Christmas lights. Have a box of Christmas tree ornaments near the tree. As the children lead the congregation in singing "O, Christmas Tree," invite members of the congregation to come up and hang an ornament on the tree. Do this on the first Sunday of Advent.

 ## BULLETIN BOARD: HELP US DECORATE OUR TREE

Instructions are on page 44.

ACTIVITY: SPONGE PAINT A CHRISTMAS TREE

MATERIALS

One big Christmas tree cut out from a large piece of white butcher paper
Tape
Green and brown tempera paints
Sponges
Scissors
Pie tins

PREPARATION

- Tape the cut-out tree to a large table.
- Put the green and brown paints into separate pie tins.

DIRECTIONS

- Demonstrate proper sponge painting technique. Dip the sponge into the paint, taking a small amount of paint each time you dip. Carefully, blot and then lift the sponge onto the tree. Do not rub the sponge on the paper (blot, lift, blot, lift, blot, lift).
- Choose one or two children to sponge paint the trunk of the tree brown. Let them take the sponge and carefully make the tree trunk go all the way to the top. As they get closer to the top of the tree, the trunk should become narrower.
- Let the rest of the children take turns sponge painting the entire tree green. Leave the bottom part of the trunk brown. It's okay to have some of the green paint obscure the trunk that runs up the tree to the top. That will give your tree a more authentic look.
- Let the tree dry. It will later be displayed in the narthex of your church.

CRAFT: A CHRISTMAS GIFT

MATERIALS

One small artificial Christmas tree per child
One cool glue gun per child
One cool glue gun stick per child
Ten to fifteen miniature Christmas ornaments per child
One gift bag and one gift tag per child
Stapler, staples
Red and green thin-tipped markers

DIRECTIONS

- Give each child a tree and a package of miniature ornaments.
- Let the children use the cool glue gun to attach their ornaments to the tree.
- Have each child put the completed tree into the gift bag and staple it shut. Give each child a gift tag and a marker and let them print their parents' names on the tag.
- Tell the kids to put their gifts under their own Christmas tree and let the parents open it when the family opens Christmas gifts.

NOTE: Be aware of the different family situations of the children in your group. Children whose parents are separated may need to make two trees. Other children may choose to give their trees to another family member.

BULLETIN BOARD: HELP US DECORATE OUR TREE

MATERIALS

The sponge-painted Christmas tree that was made by the children (p. 43)

A box filled with paper cutouts of Christmas symbols

Thin-tipped black, green, and red markers

Tape or another adhesive that will allow you to attach the tree to a wall in your narthex

One letter-sized piece of white cardstock paper

PREPARATION

- Hang the sponge-painted Christmas tree in the narthex.
- Place the box of paper cutouts near the tree.
- Use the cardstock paper to create a sign that explains the symbolism of the Christmas tree. Be sure to credit the children for creating and sharing it.

DIRECTIONS

- Invite each person in your congregation to write a Christmas message on a paper ornament of their choice.
- Let each person tape the ornament to the tree.

BULLETIN BOARD ILLUSTRATION

BONUS PUZZLE: WHAT DOES JESUS PROMISE TO GIVE US?

These words are missing some letters. Fill in the missing letters to complete the words. What's the message the missing letters help to spell out?

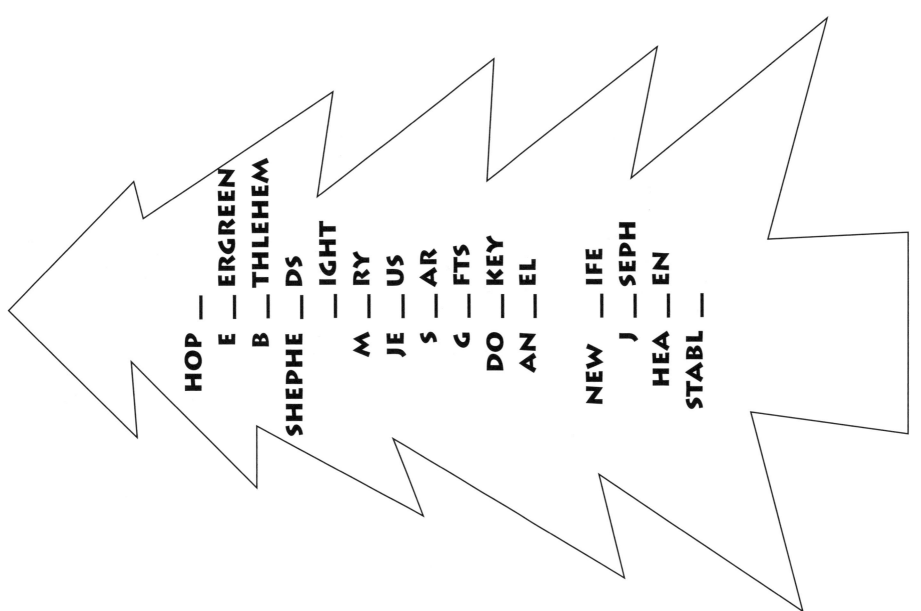

HOP __

E __ ERGREEN

B __ THLEHEM

SHEPHE __ DS

__ IGHT

M __ RY

JE __ US

S __ AR

G __ FTS

DO __ KEY

AN __ EL

NEW __ IFE

J __ SEPH

HEA __ EN

STABL __

BONUS PUZZLE SOLUTION: WHAT DOES JESUS PROMISE TO GIVE US?

These words are missing some letters. Fill in the missing letters to complete the words. What's the message the missing letters help to spell out?

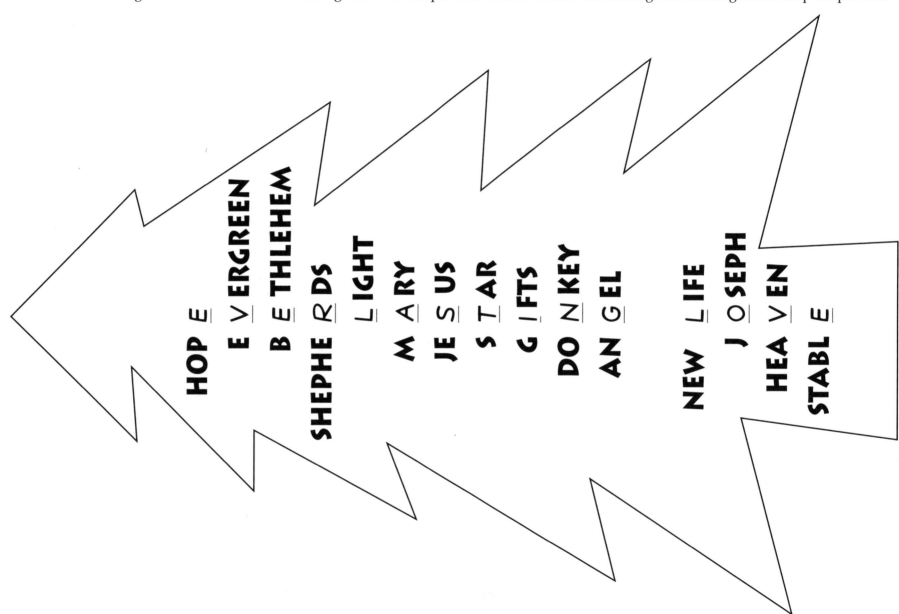

HOP E

E V ERGREEN

B ETHLEHEM

SHEPHE RDS

L IGHT

M ARY

JE S US

S T AR

G IFTS

DO N KEY

AN GEL

NEW L IFE

J O SEPH

HEA V EN

STABL E

WEEK 2: THE CANDY CANE

 SCRIPTURE: LUKE 2:8-20

Key Verse (Luke 2:8): In that region there were shepherds living in the fields, keeping watch over their flock by night.

 THEME

God's love is strong, sweet, and powerful.

 SOMETHING SPECIAL

Read the Bible story first then read this book to the children:
The Legend of the Candy Cane by Lori Walburg

 DISCUSSION

Have a large candy cane to show the children. Let them see how it can be the letter "J" for Jesus or a shepherd's staff. Talk about the white color that represents the purity of Jesus. Look at the three red stripes. The color red reminds us of the blood Jesus shed for us, and the three stripes represent the Trinity. The sweetness lets us know that God's love is sweet. Discuss how the birth of Jesus allows for all of this to be true. Explain that the shepherds were in the fields tending their sheep on the night that Jesus was born. They were using their staffs to keep the sheep in line. Sheep are not very smart, and the shepherd must use his staff to keep them from wandering away. Sometimes a sheep will fall off a cliff, and the shepherd has to pull it to safety with the staff. The shepherds care for their sheep and want to help them and keep them safe. Jesus loves us and wants to help us and keep us safe too.

 SONG

"Love Came Down at Christmas" by Christina Rossetti
You can find this song in *Around the Christmas Tree*.

 GAME: CANDY CANE RELAY

Instructions are on page 48.

 CRAFT: BEADED CANDY CANE ORNAMENTS

Instructions are on page 48.

 WORSHIP TIE-IN: A TREAT FROM JESUS

Let the children do this for congregational worship. Purchase six large candy cane decorations. Ask six children to hold the candy canes up high. Each child can tell something different about the candy cane.

One child will say, "When the candy cane is held this way, it makes the letter J for Jesus."

The next child will say, "If you turn it like this, it looks like a shepherd's staff."

The third child will say, "The white color on the candy cane reminds us of the purity of God's love."

The fourth child will say, "The red reminds us of Jesus' blood."

The fifth child will say, "The three stripes remind us of the Trinity."

The sixth child will say, "The candy cane is hard to represent the strength of God's love for us."

Have the children's choir sing the song "Love Came Down at Christmas" while some of the children pass out baskets of small candy canes. Ask the ushers to assist. Each member of the congregation can take a candy cane from the basket. The other children can hang beaded candy cane ornaments on the tree near the altar.

 BULLETIN BOARD

Add a few beaded candy cane ornaments to the tree in the narthex.

GAME: CANDY CANE RELAY

MATERIALS

Lots of large red and white balloons
White butcher paper
Red markers
Scissors
Book tape and masking tape
Laminating machine and film or clear contact paper

PREPARATION

- Blow up the balloons.
- Draw two large candy canes on the butcher paper. If you have a large group, you might need to accommodate more than two teams.
- Cut out and laminate each candy cane. Attach each candy cane to the wall.
- Use masking tape to tape a start line on the floor. If necessary, you can also tape running lanes.
- Put rolled tape on the back of each balloon.

DIRECTIONS

- Divide the kids into two teams (more teams if you have a large group). If you do not have the same number of children on each team, some children may have to run twice.
- Give each child a balloon. Alternate red and white on each team.
- Have each team form a straight line that begins at the start line.
- On the word "Go," the first child on each team runs up and sticks their balloon at the bottom of their team's candy cane that is taped to the wall. That child runs back and tags the next child who will do the same thing.
- The first team to complete their candy cane wins.
- Each member of the winning team wins a candy cane.

CRAFT: BEADED CANDY CANE ORNAMENTS

MATERIALS

Ten white beads and ten red beads per child
One 10-inch length of thin, bendable white craft wire per child
One 6-inch piece of thin red ribbon per child

PREPARATION

- Twist one end of each wire so the beads will stay on it and not slip off.
- Place one piece of craft wire, ten red beads, ten white beads, and the ribbon into a small plastic sandwich bag. Make one bag per child.

DIRECTIONS

- Give each child the bag of craft materials.
- Instruct the children to slide the beads on the craft wire—red/white, red/white—until all of the beads are used. Make sure the bent end is at the bottom. Help the children twist the wire at the top, so the beads will stay on it.
- Have the children bend the wire into a candy cane shape. Let the children tie the red ribbon on the candy cane so it can be hung. The children can use the plastic bag to carry their candy canes home. These can be hung on their Christmas trees.
- Have the kids make some extra ornaments to hang on the sanctuary and narthex trees.

BONUS PUZZLE: A SWEET TREAT

Color: R=Red, W=White, and B=Blue

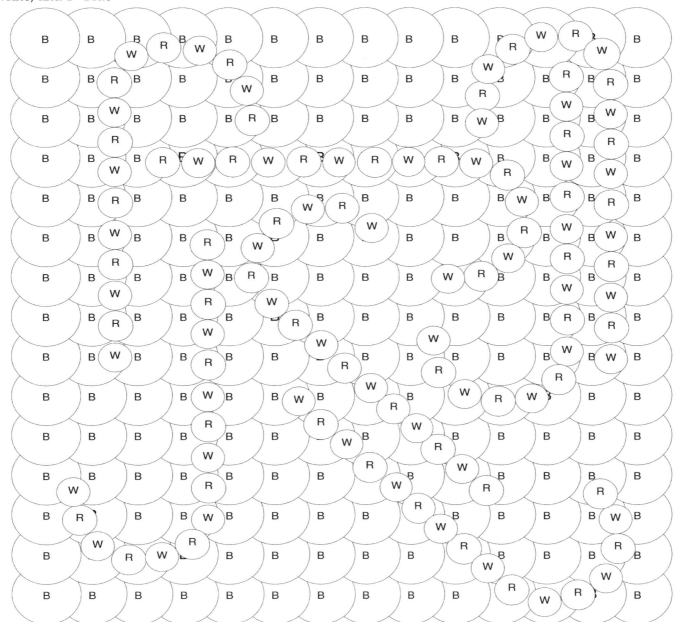

BONUS PUZZLE SOLUTION: A SWEET TREAT

Color: R=Red, W=White, and B=Blue

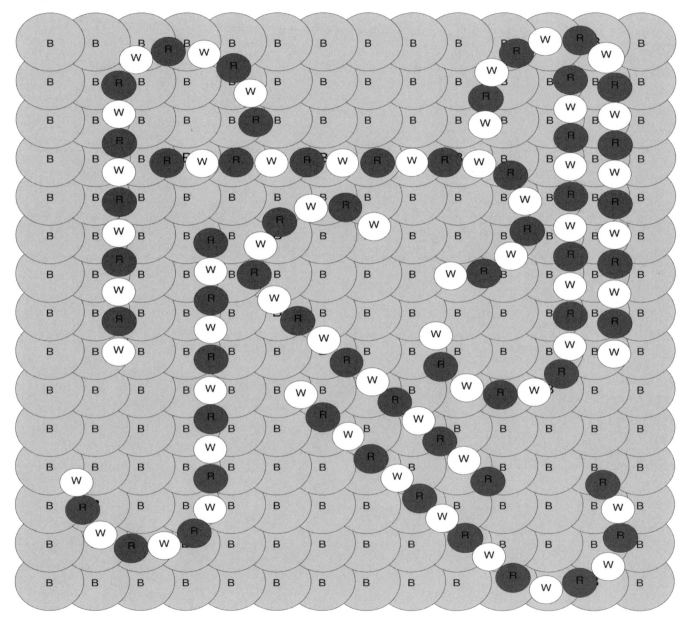

WEEK 3: THE CHRISTMAS WREATH

 ## SCRIPTURE: PSALM 5

Key Verse (Psalm 5:12 NIV): "For surely O LORD, you bless the righteous; you surround them with your favor as with a shield."

 ## THEME

God forms a continuous circle of love around us. We are loved by our family, our church family, and our friends.

 ## SOMETHING SPECIAL

Invite the children to help you create your own story about the Christmas wreath. Write it down as they dictate it to you.

 ## DISCUSSION

Explain that a circle has no beginning and no end. It's never ending, just like God's love for us is never ending. All of us are enclosed in God's continuous circle of love.

 ## SONG

"Spirit Song" by John Wimber
Teach this song to the children. You can find it in *The Praise and Worship Fake Book,* as well as some hymnals.

 ## ACTIVITY: HAND PRINT WREATH

Instructions are on pages 51-52.

 ## CRAFT: TISSUE PAPER WREATH

Instructions are on page 52.

 ## WORSHIP TIE-IN: A CIRCLE OF LOVE

Explain to the congregation that the children are learning about the Christmas wreath. The wreath is green to remind us of God's everlasting love. The roundness of the circle reminds us that we are always enclosed in God's never-ending love. Share the story that you and the children created. Give each child a green balloon that has been attached to a long thin stick. Have the children stand in a circle around the congregation and hold their green balloons up high. As the congregation sings "Spirit Song" by John Wimber, the children can walk around them. The congregation will be enveloped in the children's circle of love. Have some of the older children hang the tissue paper wreaths on the tree by the altar.

 ## BULLETIN BOARD

Hang some extra tissue paper wreaths on the tree in the narthex.

 ## ACTIVITY: HAND PRINT WREATH

MATERIALS
One extra large piece of white butcher paper or poster board
Green tempera paint
Scissors
Pie tins
Soap, water, and paper towels
Paintbrushes
A red bow
Tape

PREPARATION
- Cut out a wreath shape from the paper or white poster board.
- Pour the green paint into pie tins.

DIRECTIONS

- Let each child paint one of his or her hands green. Try to have the same number of left and right hands.
- Let the children make green handprints on the wreath (four prints per child). Caution children *not* to rub their hands on the paper. "Put your hand down, and lift it up."
- Let the wreath dry flat on the table overnight.
- When the wreath is dry, add the red bow.
- Display the wreath near the sponge-painted Christmas tree. If desired, put photos of the children inside the center of the wreath.

 CRAFT: TISSUE PAPER WREATH

MATERIALS

One 6-inch diameter cardboard circle, with the center cut out, per child
Green and red tissue paper squares (more green than red)
One 6-inch piece of red ribbon per child
Glue

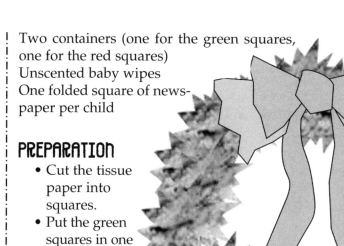

Two containers (one for the green squares, one for the red squares)
Unscented baby wipes
One folded square of news-paper per child

PREPARATION

- Cut the tissue paper into squares.
- Put the green squares in one container and the red squares in another container.
- Tie the red rib-bons into bows.

DIRECTIONS

- Give each child a folded newspaper square to work on.
- Give each child a cardboard circle and a bottle of glue. Let the kids use their fingers to smear the glue onto the cardboard circle. A thin layer of glue is all that is needed.
- Have the children clean their hands with the unscented baby wipes.
- Give each child a handful of green squares and a few red squares.
- Tell the children to squish each square into a loose ball. Put the squished squares onto the glue and push down gently. Mix in red squares with the green squares, so it looks like there are red berries on the wreath.
- Give each child a red bow to glue to the wreath.
- Let the kids carry their wreaths home on the newspaper squares. The wreaths can be hung on their Christmas trees.

 BULLETIN BOARD

Hang a few extra tissue paper wreaths on the narthex tree.

BONUS PUZZLE: GOD'S CIRCLE OF LOVE

Cross out the word "God" every time you find it in the puzzle. When you are finished, you'll find a message.

START

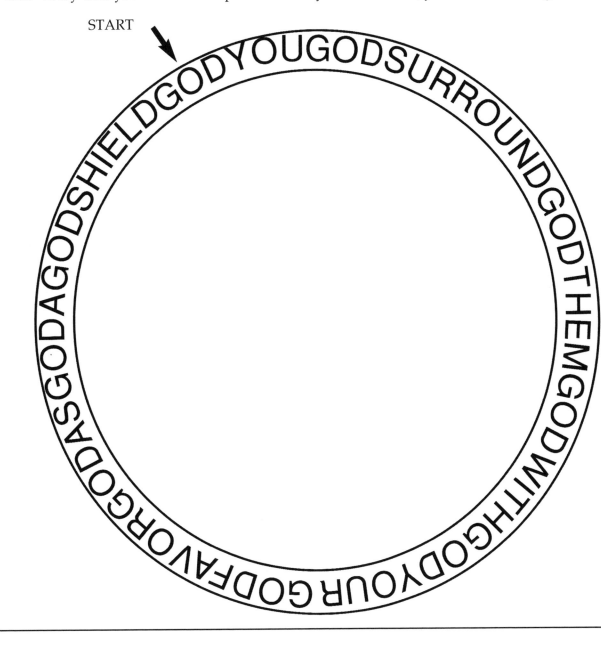

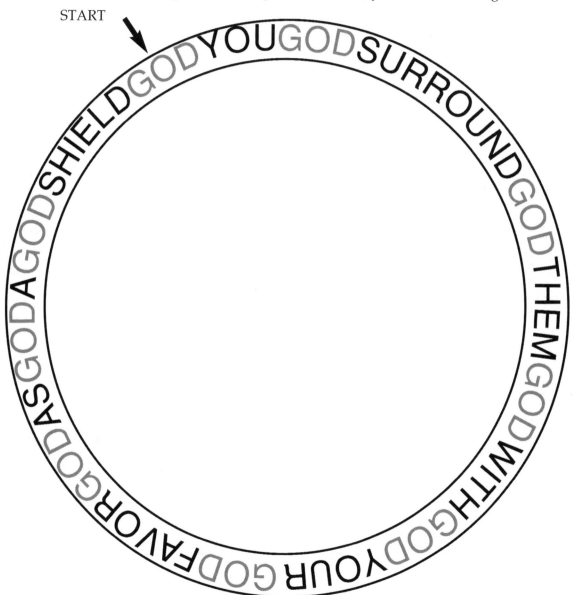 BONUS PUZZLE SOLUTION: GOD'S CIRCLE OF LOVE

Cross out the word "God" every time you find it in the puzzle. When you are finished, you'll find a message.

START

YOU SURROUND THEM WITH YOUR FAVOR AS A SHIELD

WEEK 4: THE ANGELS

 SCRIPTURE: MATTHEW 1:18-25; LUKE 1:26-38; LUKE 2:8-20

Key Verse (Luke 2:14): "Glory to God in the highest heaven, and on earth peace among those whom he favors!"

 THEME

God has interesting and good ways of getting our attention.

 STORY

In your own words, tell of the three visits the angels made. Tell how the angel Gabriel visited Mary, how an angel visited Joseph, and how the angels announced the birth of Jesus to the shepherds.

 DISCUSSION

Explain that angels were very important messengers sent by God. They gave three messages about Jesus. Gabriel, the angel with the first message, told Mary that she would be the mother of Jesus. The second angel told Joseph that he would be the earthly father of Jesus, and the third angel's message announced the arrival of Jesus to the shepherds. Ask the children why they think God sent angels to deliver the three messages about the birth of Jesus. Do you think that was the only way God could relay the messages? Remind the children that the world did not have television, phones, or radios back in those days.

 ACTIVITY: ANGEL COOKIES

Instructions are on page 56.

 SONG

"Hark, the Herald Angels Sing"

Teach the children to sing this song. It can be found in most church hymnals.

 CRAFT: ANGEL ORNAMENTS

Instructions are on pages 56-57.

 WORSHIP TIE-IN: GOD'S MESSENGERS

Choose three children who are willing to speak before the congregation. Have them dress in angel costumes. Each child can represent a different angel.

The first angel will say, "I am Gabriel. I was the angel who visited Mary and told her she would give birth to God's son, Jesus. She was really surprised, but I told her that God really wanted her to be the mother of Jesus."

The second child will say, "I am the angel who visited Joseph. I told him that it was OK for him and Mary to get married. I explained that the baby Mary was carrying was God's son, Jesus. I told him that he would be Jesus' earthly father."

The third child can say, "I am the angel who announced the birth of Jesus to the shepherds. They were really scared, but I told them that Jesus was their Savior and that there was nothing to be afraid of!"

Select other children to hold dowel rods with long, shiny gold streamers attached. They can surround the congregation by standing in the aisles (center and sides) as well as standing across the back and front of the sanctuary.

Ask your children's choir to lead the congregation in singing "Hark, the Herald Angels Sing." As everyone is singing, the children holding the dowel rods with the gold streamers can wave them around. Let some of the children add the angel ornaments to the tree by the altar.

BULLETIN BOARD: OUR CHRISTMAS ANGELS

Instructions are on page 57.

ACTIVITY: ANGEL COOKIES

MATERIALS

Several packages of ready-to-bake
  sugar cookie dough
Several angel cookie cutters
Gold sprinkles
Preheated oven
Several baking sheets
Baking flour
Parchment paper
Powdered hot chocolate mix
Whipped cream
Paper napkins
Paper cups
Spatula
Liquid hand sanitizer

PREPARATION

- Preheat oven according to the directions given with the cookie dough.
- Prepare baking sheets according to the directions given with the cookie dough.
- Place a 12" x 12" piece of parchment by each child's place at the table.

DIRECTIONS

- Have children use hand sanitizer before handling the dough.
- Give each child a large slice of the cookie dough.
- Have the children use their hands to flatten the dough until it is the desired thickness. (Use the directions that come with the cookie dough as your guide.)
- Let the children use the angel cookie cutters to cut an angel out of their dough. Have the kids sprinkle gold sprinkles on their angels.

- Place the angels on the baking sheet and bake them according to the directions on the package.
- Let the kids enjoy warm angel cookies and hot chocolate with whipped cream.
- Relate the warm, sweet cookies and hot chocolate to the warm feelings we get when we remember Jesus.

HINT: The kids may find it easier to work with the dough if you lightly flour their hands.

CRAFT: ANGEL ORNAMENTS

Do this craft while the cookies are baking.

MATERIALS

One gold paper cup per child (3" diameter, 4" tall)
Three 9" x 5½" pieces of white tissue paper per child
Gold glitter glue
Stapler with staples
One white Styrofoam ball per child (should cover base of cup)
One shiny gold pipe cleaner per child (4" long)
Two small, black-tipped straight pins per child
One pink-tipped straight pin per child
One wooden craft stick per child
Hot glue gun with glue sticks

DIRECTIONS

- Give each child one Styrofoam ball and the straight pins. Let them stick two black pins into the balls to make eyes and one pink pin to make the nose.
- Give each child the tissue paper and let them decorate it (lightly) with gold glitter.
- Have the children bunch the tissue paper together in the middle and staple it to make wings. Staple the wings to the back of the cup. Secure the wings with hot glue.
- Give each child the wooden craft stick. Have them poke the stick into the ball, making sure the facial features are in the proper position. Next, they should poke the stick into the bottom of the cup so the head rests on it.

- Give each child one gold pipe cleaner. Have them twist the top of the pipe cleaner into a halo. Let the kids poke the pipe cleaner into the cup bottom behind the angel's head. The halo should go over the angel's head.
- Drizzle a small drop of hot glue around the inserted head and halo. This will keep them in place.
- Let the children take their angels home. Tell the children their angels can *sit* on the branch of their Christmas trees.
- Make some extra angels. Some of the children can add these to the tree in the sanctuary as part of the Worship Tie-in.

BULLETIN BOARD: OUR CHRISTMAS ANGELS

MATERIALS
White butcher paper to cover the bulletin board
Blue, red, green, and gold shiny Christmas wrapping paper
Pushpins
Black markers
White labels
Angel pattern (use die-cutting machine and angel die-cut pattern if available)
Letter stencils (use die-cutting machine if available)
Scissors

PREPARATION AND DIRECTIONS
- Cover the bulletin board with white paper.
- Cut out a bunch of angel patterns from the green, red, and gold paper.
- Cut out the title OUR CHRISTMAS ANGELS from the blue paper and attach it to the board.
- Make a sign that explains that children can *purchase* angels. Green angels are $1.00, red angels are $2.50, and gold angels are $5.00. Children should be encouraged to use their own money for this project rather than relying on parents to subsidize it.
- Let each child who purchases an angel write their name on a white label and attach it to the appropriate colored angel.
- Use the money you raise to purchase toys for needy children in your town.
- Explain that we, like God's angels, can bring hope and joy to others.

BULLETIN BOARD ILLUSTRATION

BONUS PUZZLE: SPECIAL MESSENGERS

Complete the crossword puzzle. Print the circled letters in the blank spaces below to decipher the message.

Print the circled letters in the correct spaces.

God sometimes sends ___ ___ ___ ___ ___ ___ to give us messages from him.

ACROSS

1. Angels are ___ from God.
2. An angel told ___ that he was to be the earthly father of Jesus.
3. Jesus was born to save us from our ___.
4. ___ was visited by an angel who told her she was to be the mother of Jesus.

DOWN

1. ___ was the angel who visited Mary.
2. ___ is our Savior.
3. Jesus was born in ___.
4. The angels sang ___ to God!

BONUS PUZZLE SOLUTION: SPECIAL MESSENGERS

Complete the crossword puzzle. Print the circled letters in the blank spaces below to decipher the message.

Print the circled letters in the correct spaces.

God sometimes sends <u>A</u> <u>N</u> <u>G</u> <u>E</u> <u>L</u> <u>S</u> to give us messages from him.

ACROSS
1. Angels are ___ from God.
2. An angel told ___ that he was to be the earthly father of Jesus.
3. Jesus was born to save us from our ___.
4. ___ was visited by an angel who told her she was to be the mother of Jesus.

DOWN
1. ___ was the angel who visited Mary.
2. ___ is our Savior.
3. Jesus was born in ___.
4. The angels sang ___ to God!

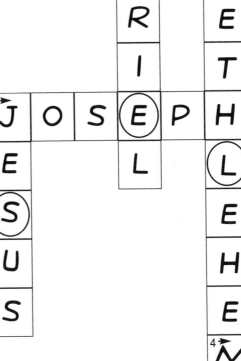

WEEK 5: HE'S ARRIVED!

This program celebrates the birth of Jesus. Rent or make a large lawn sign that says, "We are pleased to announce the birth of our Savior, Jesus Christ, who was born December 25, in a stable in Bethlehem. Come on in to greet this newborn baby!" Have your Christmas worship times printed on the sign. Place the sign in front of your church.

Hang large glittery stars from the ceiling of your room. At the far end, construct a stable with a large Bethlehem star hanging above it. Have a manger with a real baby or life-like baby doll in it. Ask two members of your youth group to dress as and portray Mary and Joseph. Have other members of the youth group dress as and portray shepherds. Ask an adult man to portray the innkeeper.

Have stuffed animals to represent the animals (sheep, cows, dove) in the stable.

Darken the room as much as possible. Have Mary, Joseph, Jesus, and the shepherds in place before the children arrive. Let the children enter the room and find this scene. Let them react. It's fine if they go up to the scene in excitement. It's also acceptable if they stay back and just observe.

Work with your actors prior to the program, so they are prepared to present a brief dramatization. Mary can tell how the angel came to her to announce that she would be the mother of Jesus. Joseph can explain how the angel came to tell him he would be the earthly father of Jesus. Both Mary and Joseph can talk about their journey to Bethlehem to register for the census. The innkeeper can explain that he just didn't have room at the inn. The shepherds can share how the angels told them about the birth of Jesus. Work together to write your own script, and practice it ahead of time so everyone is well prepared.

 ## SCRIPTURE: LUKE 2:1-20

Key Verse (Luke 2:10): But the angel said to them, "Do not be afraid; for see—I am bringing you good news of great joy for all the people: to you is born this day in the city of David a Savior, who is the Messiah, the Lord."

 ## THEME

Our Lord and Savior, Jesus, has been born! God sent Jesus to save us from sin.

 ## SOMETHING SPECIAL

Have your youth group present the story of the birth of Jesus. See the introductory material at the beginning of this lesson.
—or—
Read either of these stories aloud:
A Child Was Born by Grace Maccarone
A Child Is Born by Margaret Wise Brown

 ## DISCUSSION

Ask the children what it was like to walk into the room and find baby Jesus in the stable. Did you expect to find that today? Were you surprised? Talk about the story. Explain that Jesus was sent by God to be our Savior. God had tried very hard to tell people how they were supposed to behave, but they just didn't get it! So God decided to send someone to earth to help us understand how God wants us to live.

God thought about it for a long time, and he decided to send a tiny, helpless baby, who would be a child just like you. God wanted Jesus to live life as people do. God wanted Jesus to have parents and a home. God wanted Jesus to experience many of the same things we all experience. But most important, God wanted Jesus to set an example of how we should behave. Therefore, Jesus would live without sinning! Wow! That must be really hard to do. Live without sinning? Do you think you could live without ever doing anything wrong?

God wanted Jesus to teach us lessons about living life the way God wants us to live. God wanted Jesus to help us learn all of the lessons the Lord wants us to learn. God had special plans for Jesus, plans that would allow Jesus to make learning about God interesting and enjoyable.

But God also had another plan for Jesus. God wanted Jesus to be our Savior. God decided that Jesus would have to pay for all of our sins. He would have to be crucified and die on the cross. Jesus would take all of

 60

our sins with him when he died. Then Jesus would be resurrected to prove that there is *new life*. That's how much God loves us. God was willing to give us his very own son so that we could be forgiven for our sins. WOW! That's truly amazing, isn't it?

Talk about some of the names we use to describe Jesus: Savior, Teacher, Counselor, Friend, Prince of Peace.

When you discuss the birth of Jesus with the children, keep in mind that the children's various ages and levels of development will be reflected in their understanding and discussion.

Reassure the children that Jesus came to show how much God loves us.

GAME: ALL THOSE ANIMALS AT THE MANGER

Instructions are on pages 61-62.

SONG

"He's Arrived" (*"If You're Happy"*)
He's arrived, and we're happy as can be! (*clap, clap*)
He's arrived, and we're happy as can be! (*clap, clap*)
He's arrived, and we're happy!
He's arrived, and we're happy!
He's arrived, and we're happy as can be! (*clap, clap*)

He's our Savior, and we're joyful as can be! (*stamp, stamp*)
He's our Savior, and we're joyful as can be! (*stamp, stamp*)
He's our Savior, and we're joyful!
He's our Savior, and we're joyful!
He's our Savior, and we're joyful as can be! (*stamp, stamp*)

CRAFT: JESUS IS A STAR

Instructions are on pages 62-63.

WORSHIP TIE-IN: HE'S ARRIVED, AND WE'RE HAPPY!

Teach the song "He's Arrived" to the children and let them sing it for family worship on Christmas Eve. Let some children carry dowel rods with colorful streamers and glittery silver stars attached. Have them wave the rods as they sing. Let others toss shiny, colorful confetti at the congregation, and let others play rhythm instruments. If possible, have the children surround the congregation. Print the words in the bulletin, and invite the congregation to sing along.

BULLETIN BOARD: BIRTH ANNOUNCEMENT

Instructions are on page 63.

GAME: ALL THOSE ANIMALS AT THE MANGER

MATERIALS
White butcher paper
Tempera paints and paint brushes
Colorful patterns for barn animals (cows, sheep, donkeys, hens, chicks, roosters, doves, dogs, cats, horses, owls, bugs)
Laminating machine and film (or clear contact paper)
Scissors
Clear book tape
Color copier
Blindfold
Basket

PREPARATION

- Use the tempera paints to paint a manger scene on the white butcher paper. Draw Mary, Joseph, and baby Jesus in the manger. Let this dry for a couple of days. Laminate it.
- Tape the picture to the wall.
- Make a color copy of the animal pictures then laminate them. Cut them out. Place them in a basket.

DIRECTIONS

- This is played like "Pin the Tail on the Donkey."
- Blindfold each child before handing him or her an animal to add to the scene. Let each child have a turn at adding the animals to the manger scene. Put a rolled piece of book tape on the back of each animal as you hand it to the child. If they do not know what animal they have, you might end up with a very interesting picture. Caution the other children *not* to tell the others what animals they are putting into the scene.

CRAFT: JESUS IS A STAR

MATERIALS

Silver cardboard (or poster board)
Colored shiny cardboard (red, green, blue, gold, orange, purple)
Thin silver ribbon
Scissors
Hole puncher
Large and small labels

PREPARATION

- Cut out one large star from the silver board per child.
- Cut out five smaller colored stars per child. Each child should receive five different colored stars.
- Type the name JESUS in a large font onto large labels. Make one JESUS label per child.
- Type the words: SAVIOR, TEACHER, FRIEND, COUNSELOR, and PRINCE OF PEACE onto smaller labels using a smaller font. Make one set of these labels per child.
- Type the Bible verse onto a set of large labels. Make one Bible verse label per child.
- Cut one 24-inch strand of silver ribbon per child.
- Cut five additional silver strands of ribbon per child. Vary the lengths of each ribbon (6, 8, 10, 12, and 14 inches).
- Punch one hole into the top and bottom of each silver star.
- Punch one hole into the top of each colored star.

DIRECTIONS

- Give each child the large silver star, the 24-inch piece of ribbon, the JESUS label, and the Bible verse label. Have each child stick the JESUS label to one side of the star and the Bible verse label to the other side of the star. Have each child attach the 24-inch

STAR PATTERN

strand of silver ribbon through the hole at the top of the silver star, and tie the ribbon in a knot at the top.

- Give each child the five color stars (one of each color) and the set of five name labels. Have them stick one name label on each star.
- Give the children the five additional pieces of silver ribbon. Have them string one ribbon through each star, and tie the ribbon in a knot by the hole in the star. Have the children gather all five strings of ribbon. All ends should be even. Have the children slip the ribbons through the hole at the bottom of the large silver star. Tie the ribbons in a knot.

BULLETIN BOARD: BIRTH ANNOUNCEMENT

MATERIALS

Several shades of 12-inch blue paper squares
One large piece of white poster board
Dark blue cardstock paper
Letter stencils (use die-cutting machine if available)
Scissors
Pushpins
Black marker
Red marker
Small baby items (rattles, pacifiers, booties)
Ribbon
Glue
Blue yarn

PREPARATION

- Cover the board with the squares of colored blue paper. Alternate the colors, so it looks like a patchwork quilt design.

- Laminate the dark blue cardstock paper. Cut out letters that say BIRTH ANNOUNCEMENT.
- Cut the white poster board to fit the bulletin board. Glue the title BIRTH ANNOUNCEMENT to the white poster board. Make the poster into a birth announcement (see sample below).
- Attach the birth announcement to the bulletin board.
- Attach yarn to each of the baby items and place them into a basket.

DIRECTIONS

- Explain that parents often send out birth announcements when they welcome a new baby into their home. Talk about why parents would want to do this.
- Let each child have a turn at attaching one of the baby items to the board.

BULLETIN BOARD ILLUSTRATION

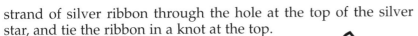

BONUS PUZZLE: WHO IS JESUS?

Fill in the missing letters to complete these words that have to do with Jesus. Print the letters you used here to reveal a special message.

___ ___ ___ ___ ___   ___ ___   ___ ___ ___   ___ ___ ___ ___ ___ ___ ___!

___EWISH

DISCIPL___S

GOD'S ___ON

P___RE

CROS___

ETERNAL L___FE

___TRONG

PRINCE ___F PEACE

R___LER

F___IEND

JO___EPH

C___RING

E___ERLASTING LOVE

M___GHTY

SAVI___R

TEACHE___

BONUS PUZZLE SOLUTION: WHO IS JESUS?

Fill in the missing letters to complete these words that have to do with Jesus. Print the letters you used here to reveal a special message.

JESUS IS OUR SAVIOR

J EWISH

DISCIPL E S

GOD'S S ON

P U RE

CROS S

ETERNAL L I FE

S TRONG

PRINCE O F PEACE

R U LER

F R IEND

JO S EPH

C A RING

E V ERLASTING LOVE

M I GHTY

SAVI O R

TEACHE R

THE KINGS ARE COMING

SONSATIONAL SUNDAY CELEBRATION

Offer this program to children and their parents on Epiphany Sunday. If possible, combine all of the children in kindergarten through fifth grade and have a *Sonsational* Sunday Celebration. Use your fellowship hall or another large room in the church. This will be a time where you can share what the children learned during your Advent and Christmas workshops.

Set up the room so it becomes a Bethlehem Fair. Provide a large area rug where the children can sit for the story-sharing portion of the program. Have chairs around and behind the rug for the parents.

You will have six booths set up in different areas of the room: The Gathering Place, Advent Wreath Ring Toss, Christmas Tree Booth, Candy Cane Bake Shop, Three Gifts at the Stable, and The Wise Men's Resting Place. Have a different activity at each booth. These are all simple to set up and do. Have inexpensive prizes at each booth such as stickers, hand stamps, and tattoos.

Parents and children can *travel* from one activity to another. Have two Sunday school teachers who will be responsible for each booth and setting up their activities. They will help the children and parents talk about what they have learned throughout the Advent and Christmas seasons at each booth. They will also give out prizes to each child who visits and participates in the activity at each booth.

Give each child a white lunch sack for carrying prizes. Let them use green or red markers to write their names on the bag. Kids can use stickers, stamps, and markers to decorate their bags if desired.

Decorate the room with the group artwork done by the children each week. Put the appropriate artwork by each booth (for example, Wreaths with the Advent Wreath Ring Toss Booth). Post signs that explain each of the holiday symbols you discovered during Advent and Christmas. Encourage the children to show off the artwork to their parents.

Ask three men in your congregation to help you by dressing as and portraying the wise men. They can enter at the beginning of the program and listen to you share the story. They can wander about the Bethlehem Fair and talk to the children and parents.

Let parents and kids know that this is a "casual and comfy" dress day. Dress to play and be messy! Another idea is to let the kids don the Bible costumes (See p. xii).

See pages 68-69 for each booth's instructions.

Begin the program by having everyone sit in the Gathering Place (kids on the rug with parents on the chairs).

 ## SCRIPTURE: MATTHEW 2:1-12

Key Verse (Matthew 2:2 NIV): "We saw his star in the east and have come to worship him."

 ## THEME

It's important to follow and worship Jesus. Jesus wants gifts from our hearts rather than gifts we buy.

 ## SOMETHING SPECIAL

Read this book aloud:
The Legend of Old Befana by Tomie dePaola

 ## DISCUSSION

Discuss the story of the three wise men coming to visit Jesus. Have props on hand so the children and parents can actually experience the gold, incense, and myrrh. Explain that the gold was a gift to give to a king. Jesus was a king. Explain that the incense was a gift for someone worthy of worship. We worship Jesus. In some churches incense is still used to show honor for God. The myrrh was a spice for a man who would die. Explain that when Jesus died on the cross, the women went to the tomb to put myrrh on his body. That's how Jewish people paid their respect to those who died.

Ask the children what it must have been like for the wise men. They rode lumpy, bumpy camels all the way. When did they travel? Day or night? Why? Explain that it took the wise men two years to arrive in Bethlehem. It was a long and hard journey by lumpy, bumpy camels.

Tell the children that we do not know for sure how many wise men there were. The Bible tells us that they brought three gifts, but it does not say how many wise men. What do you think the wise men did when they stopped to rest? There were no motels with swimming pools, video games, DVD players, or cable TV in those days!

Talk about how Old Befana missed out on seeing baby Jesus because she was too busy. What happens if we are too busy to meet Jesus?

 ## SONG

"We Three Kings of Orient Are" by John Henry Hopkins
This can be found in most hymnals.

 ## IDEA

Hang the Christmas trees and the three gifts in the narthex so that all members of your congregation can enjoy what the children created. Mention the children's creations in your newsletter, on your weekly announcements page, in your church bulletin, or during parish announcements. Place photos on your church website. This is a good way to publicize your children's ministry program, and it might be a way to recruit volunteers to work with the children.

 ## BULLETIN BOARD: WE SAW HIS STAR

Instructions are on page 70.

 ## ACTIVITY: GOIN' TO THE BETHLEHEM FAIR

After you have sung the song together, explain that everyone will travel to the different booths at the fair. Tell a little about each booth and let people decide in which order they want to travel. Tell kids to use their white sacks to collect their travel souvenirs.

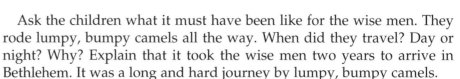

STATION 1: CHRISTMAS TREE BOOTH (PLAYED LIKE "PIN THE TAIL ON THE DONKEY")

Have large sponge-painted trees taped to the wall (see p. 43). Have a bunch of precut Christmas symbol ornaments, crayons and markers, clear book tape, Christmas tree stickers, and an eyeshade. Let the children decorate an ornament, put a piece of rolled book tape on the back of the ornaments, and let each child put on the eyeshade. Spin each child around three times, point the child in the direction of the trees, and let the child tape the ornament anywhere on the trees. When you are finished, you will have some beautifully decorated Christmas trees. While the children are at this booth, talk about the symbolism of the Christmas tree (see p. 42). Give each child a Christmas tree sticker at this booth.

STATION 2: CANDY CANE BAKE SHOP

Have this in the kitchen. Provide several rolls of ready-to-bake sugar cookie dough and a bunch of crushed up candy canes. Use a rolling pin to crush these yourself before the program. Preheat the oven to the temperature listed on the cookie dough package. Give each person one slice of cookie dough and a spoon full of crushed candy canes. Let each person work the crushed candy canes into the dough and shape the cookie so it looks like a candy cane. Put the cookies on a baking sheet, and bake the cookies according to the directions on the package. Let the kids and parents eat their freshly baked cookies. Have some premoistened towelettes for hand cleaning. Everyone should clean their hands before and after working with the cookie dough.

Talk about the symbolism of the candy cane while the kids and parents are making candy cane cookies (see p. 47). The cookies are the prizes at this booth.

STATION 3: ADVENT WREATH RING TOSS

Have a large Advent wreath sitting on the floor. Provide five rings for people to use in the ring toss game. The object is to toss each ring so it lands around a different candle. Purple candles are worth two points, the pink candle is worth five points, and the white candle is worth ten points.

Talk about each of the candles on the Advent wreath. The purple candles remind us of the royalty of Jesus. The pink candle reminds us that Jesus was human, and the white candle reminds us that Jesus is divine. Stamp each child's hand as they play the game. Talk about the symbolism of the wreath (see p. 51).

STATION 4: THREE GIFTS AT THE STABLE

Have a manger with artificial straw and a baby doll. Set up several tables. Tape together four large pieces of white construction paper for each of the three gifts. Put the tape on the back of the paper so the front will be free for writing. Use wide green, red, and purple ribbons to make the white "boxes" look like wrapped presents. Add green, red, and purple bows to each box. One will have a green ribbon and bow, one will have red, and one will have purple.

Make a gift tag for each box. Use a green marker to write "A Gift for Me" and place it on the *green* gift. Use a red marker to write "A Gift for a Friend" and tape it to the *red* gift. Use a purple marker to write "A Gift for Jesus," and tape it to the *purple* gift.

Have thin green markers with the green gift, thin red markers with the red gift, and thin purple markers with the purple gift. Each child will write something on each gift. On the green gift, they will write a gift they would like to receive; on the red gift, they will write something they would give to a friend; and on the purple gift, they will write a gift they would give to Jesus.

NOTE: **These must be gifts they cannot buy with money.** They cannot go to the store to buy the gifts. They cannot order the gifts off of the Internet or eBay; they cannot use a credit card or a debit card to buy it. This will challenge many children, but it's an excellent lesson in gifts from the heart.

Talk about the colors of Christmas at this booth. Purple reminds us of the royalty of Jesus. Red reminds us that Jesus shed his blood for us. Green reminds us that God's love is everlasting. And, white reminds us of the purity of God's love. Give each child a religious tattoo at this booth.

STATION 5: WISE MEN'S RESTING PLACE

You'll need four Twister games. Use clear book tape to tape the four game boards together to make one giant-sized Twister game. Put the tape on the back and front, so the seams are securely taped down. Place the game board on the floor. Have the kids stand along the outside circles with each foot on a different circle. Play the game as directed.

With a big batch of kids on the board, this game is loads of fun. The faster you spin the spinner and call out the moves, the more fun it becomes.

Talk about how the wise men had to journey to Bethlehem. They had to follow the directions to arrive. What indicated which direction they were to follow? Give each kid a large star sticker at this booth.

STATION 6: THE STARS CRAFT BOOTH

Have a laminated copy of the memory verse for each child. Type these ahead of time. You can fit several copies of the verse on one page of paper. Print these out, make additional copies as needed, laminate them, and cut them into individual pieces. Look for plastic stars on key rings in craft stores or catalogs (Oriental Trading Company, Michaels, Hobby

Lobby). Punch a hole in each Bible verse and slide it onto the key ring. Make the star craft according to the directions that come with the craft

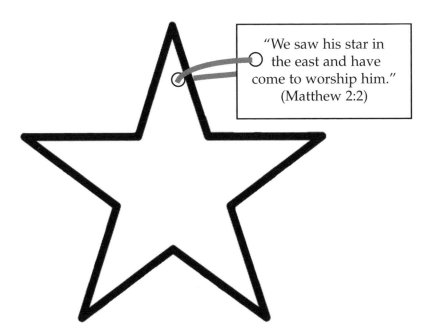

"We saw his star in the east and have come to worship him." (Matthew 2:2)

kit you are using. Talk about the meaning of the Christmas star at this booth. The star key ring is the prize at this booth.

CLOSING

Have everyone return to the Gathering Place. Thank the parents and children for coming to your *Sonsational* Sunday Celebration—Bethlehem Fair. Offer a closing prayer:

"Hey God . . . we thank you for this wonderful day we have had celebrating the birth of your awesome son, Jesus! Thank you for loving us enough to give us Jesus. Help us to remember to live our lives as Jesus wants us to live them. AMEN!"

Give each person a freshly baked angel cookie to remind them of the angels.

BULLETIN BOARD: WE SAW HIS STAR

MATERIALS

Dark blue paper large enough to cover the bulletin board
Laminating machine and film
Large piece of silver poster board
Silver Christmas wrapping paper
Pushpins
Scissors
Letter stencils (use die-cutting machine if available)
Silver gel pens

PREPARATION

- Cover the bulletin board with the blue paper.
- Cut a Bethlehem star out of the silver poster board and use the pushpins to attach it to the bulletin board.
- Use letter stencils or the die-cutting machine and letters to cut out the words: "WE SAW HIS STAR IN THE EAST AND HAVE COME TO WORSHIP HIM (MATTHEW 2:2)" out of the silver wrapping paper. (If possible laminate the silver paper before cutting the letters out. It makes the letters sturdier and easier to work with.)
- Use the pushpins to attach the title to the bulletin board.

DIRECTIONS

- Let the children use silver gel pens to write their names on the blue paper.

BULLETIN BOARD ILLUSTRATION

ANGELA   SANDY

JOHN   TARA

TED   BOBBY

WE SAW HIS STAR IN THE EAST AND HAVE COME TO WORSHIP HIM
(MATTHEW 2:2)

DANIEL   CATHY

BONUS PUZZLE SOLUTION: HELP THEM FIND THE WAY

Find the path that will lead the wise men to Jesus.

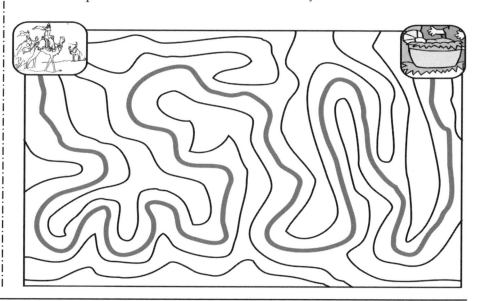

BONUS PUZZLE: HELP THEM FIND THE WAY

Find the path that will lead the wise men to Jesus.

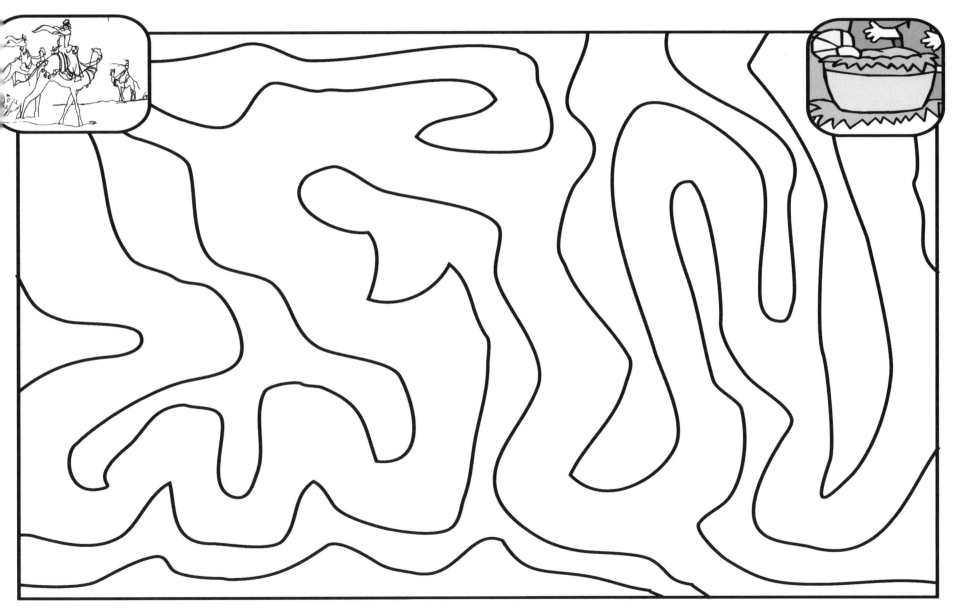

Section Three

THE FINAL WEEK

This section focuses on the final week Jesus spent on earth. Each lesson will feature a different event that occurred during Holy Week beginning with the parade on Palm Sunday and ending with the news of the Resurrection.

On Easter Sunday, you and the children will experience another *Sonsational* Sunday Celebration filled with a variety of learning experiences that tie the entire unit together. Invite the parents to be a part of this celebration, so they can share in the children's joy at hearing the good news about Jesus.

As you prepare to lead the children through the events of Holy Week, reflect upon your own journey with the Lord. Imagine what it would be like to know that this is the last week you will spend on earth. What legacy would you want to leave behind? What would you want to say to those you love? What would you be thinking and feeling? Let these thoughts and feelings guide you as you prepare to share this momentous journey of our Lord and Savior, Jesus Christ.

DAY 1: SUNDAY—IT'S A PARADE!

Read and study the four biblical versions of this story.

ROOM SETUP

Have discarded palm branches and fronds scattered about the area. Add crumpled paper and other materials that would indicate a crowd has been there.

Try to find a donkey that you can borrow. Ask a young man in your congregation to portray Jesus riding into Jerusalem on the donkey. Find a group of people to portray the parade goers in Jerusalem. Ask a young man to portray one of the disciples of Jesus. Ask others in the congregation to dress as and portray the people of Jerusalem. Have your actors hidden from view somewhere outside your building. Have them dramatize this story. The children will join them.

SCRIPTURE: MATTHEW 21:1-11; MARK 11:1-11; LUKE 19:28-44; JOHN 12:12-19

Key Verse (John 12:13): "Hosanna!
Blessed is the one who comes in the name of the Lord!"

THEME

We need to prepare a way for the Lord.

DRAMATIZATION

When the children arrive in the classroom say, "Oh you just missed it! There was a parade through here. A man came riding through on a donkey. People were shouting things like 'Hosanna! Blessed is the one who comes in the name of the Lord!' It was amazing! I couldn't see who it was on the donkey, but everyone wanted to get a look at him. Someone said it was Jesus of Nazareth, that man who goes around teaching things."

Have the disciple burst into your room saying, "Come quickly! You might be able to see him if you hurry! Jesus is coming! He asked some of us to go and get him a donkey to ride, so we did. Now Jesus is riding the donkey and the crowd is really excited to see him."

Take the children outside where they will see a group of people lined up to watch a parade. Jesus will come riding through on the donkey.

Say, "It is Jesus! And he's riding on a donkey! I wonder why?"

The people will shout. "Hosanna! Blessed is the one who comes in the name of the Lord." Jesus will ride by waving to all of the people who will keep shouting and waving back.

Hand out palms for the children to wave. Let them shout "Hosanna! Blessed is the one who comes in the name of the Lord!"

Take the children into the narthex of the sanctuary, where the congregation will experience the beginning of their Palm Sunday celebration.

WORSHIP TIE-IN: LOOK! A PARADE!

Set up this same scene for the congregation. Play the scene out the way you did it with the children. Then let the children enter the sanctuary singing, "Hosanna! Blessed is the one who comes in the name of the Lord!" while waving their palm branches. Have "Jesus" walk down the aisle among them. (Leave the donkey outside.) Invite the congregation to become a part of the parade. They can file down the center aisle, get a palm branch from a child, and parade out into the narthex and back into the sanctuary where they will return to their seats. "Jesus" will leave the sanctuary with the children. He will return to the teaching area with them.

Discussion

Once back in your teaching area, talk about what just happened. Tell the kids to pretend they are living back when Jesus lived. What was it like to actually see Jesus ride down the street? Did you expect that? Why do you think he rode into town on a donkey? Why do you think people were shouting "Hosanna! Blessed is the one who comes in the name of the Lord?" Why did the people wave palm branches? Ask "Jesus" to share his thoughts and feelings about that day.

Explain that the word *hosanna* means "God save us." The people wanted God to save them from their sins. Palm branches are a symbol of victory. Jesus would be victorious over death. The Jewish people considered a donkey an unclean animal. Jesus spent his time with those who sinned (were unclean) and came to save all sinners. Tell the children that Palm Sunday is the beginning of the final week of Jesus' life. Let them share their thoughts and feelings about this story.

 ## Something Special

Read this book to the children:
  The Colt and the King by Marni McGee

 ## Song

"Here Comes the Lord" (*"The Farmer in the Dell"*)
  Here comes the Lord!
  Here comes the Lord!
  Here comes Jesus!
  Here comes the Lord!

  He's riding a donkey!
  He's riding a donkey!
  Here comes Jesus!
  He's riding a donkey!

  They all shout hosanna!
  They all shout hosanna!
  Here comes Jesus!
  They all shout hosanna!

 ## Game: Pin the Tail on the Donkey

Find a Pin the Tail on the Donkey game and let the kids play it. Try to find a picture of Jesus to put on the donkey.

 ## Craft: Palm Prints

Instructions are on page 75.

 ## Bulletin Board: Hosanna!

Instructions are on page 76.

 ## Craft: Palm Prints

Materials
One 9" x 12" sheet of black construction paper per child
One 11" x 14" sheet of colored cardstock per child
One small palm branch per child
Colored tempera paints (blue, purple, green, yellow, orange, red)
Clean pie tins
Paintbrushes
Newspaper
Rubber cement

Preparation
• Pour a thin layer of paint into each pie tin. Each tin should have a different color of paint.

Directions
• Give each child a small palm branch.
• Let the children use the paintbrushes to *lightly* spread a *very thin* coat of paint on their branch. Each child can choose *one* color to use.
• Give each child a piece of black paper.

- Have each child carefully turn the palm branch over and place it on top of the black paper, press down lightly, and carefully lift the palm branch off of the paper. Be careful not to move the branch around.
- Let the paintings dry.
- Rubber cement each child's painting on a larger piece of colored cardstock paper.

BULLETIN BOARD: HOSANNA!

MATERIALS

Black paper
Neon colored paper (orange, yellow, and pink)
Brightly colored blue and green cardstock paper
Letter stencils (use die-cutting machine if available)
Pushpins
Pencils and thin-tipped felt markers
Scissors

PREPARATION
- Cover the board with black paper.
- Cut out the letters HOSANNA. Make three sets: yellow, orange, and pink. Attach them to the board so that they overlap.

DIRECTIONS
- Give each child a piece of green or blue cardstock paper and a pencil.
- Let each child trace a hand onto the paper. Let the children cut out their hands, sign their names to the hands, and attach them to the board.

BULLETIN BOARD ILLUSTRATION

BONUS PUZZLE: A PALM SUNDAY PARADE

Can you find these ten objects hidden in this picture: a hat, a water jug, a sandal, a loaf of bread, a fish, a basket, a sheep, a coin, a dove, and a lily.

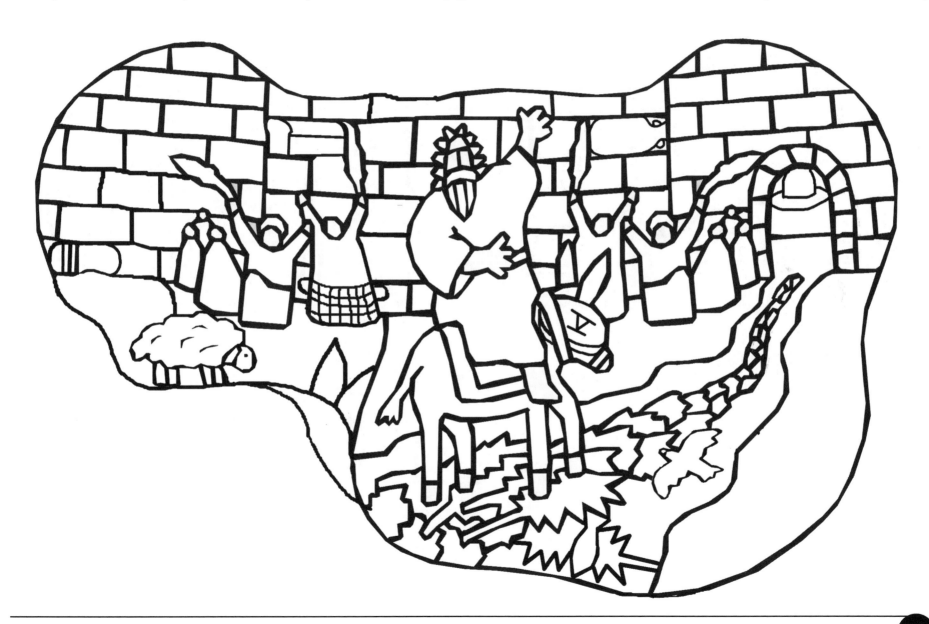

BONUS PUZZLE SOLUTION: A PALM SUNDAY PARADE

Can you find these ten objects hidden in this picture: a hat, a water jug, a sandal, a loaf of bread, a fish, a basket, a sheep, a coin, a dove, and a lily.

DAY 2: MONDAY—GET OUT! (JESUS CLEARS THE TEMPLE)

ROOM SETUP

Turn the tables and chairs over on their sides. Scatter coins, books, papers, jugs, jewelry, and other artifacts all over the room. Make it as messy as possible.

SCRIPTURE: MATTHEW 21:12-17; MARK 11:12-19; LUKE 19:45-48

Key Verse (Matthew 21:13): "My house shall be called a house of prayer."

THEME

We must respect God's house and keep it holy.

SOMETHING SPECIAL

Read all three scriptural versions of this story, and study the commentary in *The Life Application Bible* before planning your lesson.

Let the kids enter the destroyed room. Observe their reactions. Talk to them about what they are seeing. Then tell the story of how Jesus cleared the temple. Explain that people had come from all over the world to worship God during the Passover season. The merchants had set up their booths and were selling their goods inside the temple, which was not allowed. God's house is to be used for worship and prayer. The merchants also inflated their prices, so that people had to pay prices that were higher than usual. This was not right or fair.

Also, people coming from different countries had to exchange their money for local currency. When you change money from one currency to another, you have to pay what is called an exchange rate. The money-changers charged higher exchange rates on money, which allowed them to make more money. This was wrong, and it was unfair to foreigners visiting the country.

All of this made Jesus angry. People were sinning by lying, cheating, and stealing. They were not honoring God or respecting the Ten Commandments. Jesus made the merchants and money changers leave the temple.

Ask the children how they would feel if someone came into *our* church and did that? How would you feel if someone came into *your home* or *your room* and did that?

SONG

"Hear Our Prayer" (*"Michael Row the Boat Ashore"*)
> Hear our prayer Oh Lord. Alleluia.
> Let us do what pleases you. Alleluia.

ACTIVITY: FIX IT!

Talk to the children about what they can do about the situation in the room. They will certainly decide to *fix it*. Help them put the room back together the way it should be.

CRAFT: A HOUSE OF PRAYER

Instructions are on page 80.

BULLETIN BOARD: PRAYERS FOR OUR HOME

Instructions are on page 81.

✝ WORSHIP TIE-IN: WHAT HAPPENED?

Have a similar scene set up at the front of your sanctuary. The congregation will be curious, just as the children were when they found the upheaval. Have the children come up front and say to them, "Look! There's a big mess in here too! Just like the one we saw in the Sunday school area! What do you think happened here? *(Let them respond.)* Say, "Yeah, it sure looks like there were money changers here too and people selling stuff as well. What do you think Jesus would think if he walked in here and found this mess? Now, there are a bunch of people sitting out in the congregation. They've been wondering why the front of our church is in such a disarray. They aren't very happy about it either! What do you think we should tell them?" *(Let kids respond.)* Say: "You are so right! This is God's house. It is a place of worship. We should not use it for things that do not honor God. The people in that story used God's house to change money illegally, and they used it to sell stuff, and that made Jesus angry. Jesus reminded us that we must use God's house as a place of worship." Say this prayer, and let the children sing the song, "Hear Our Prayer" in response (p. 79).

Jesus, we have disappointed you when we have not obeyed you.

Response

Jesus, we have sinned against you when we have not obeyed you.

Response

We are sorry for our sins, O Lord.

Response

Please give us strength and courage to do what is right and to obey your rules.

Amen!

Response

CRAFT: A HOUSE OF PRAYER

MATERIALS
House pattern
Crayons and markers
Pencils
Roll of self-stick magnet tape

PREPARATION
- Run one copy per child of the house on white cardstock paper
- Cut magnet tape into 1-inch pieces

DIRECTIONS
- Give each child a house with the scripture verse on it. Tell them to color the house any way they want. Remind them not to color over the Bible verse.
- Tell the children to write a prayer on the back of the house.
- Give each child two strips of magnet tape and let them attach it to the back of the house.
- Kids can use their houses as refrigerator magnets.

PATTERN FOR THE HOUSE

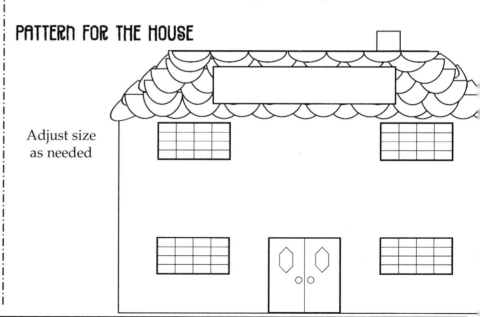

Adjust size as needed

BULLETIN BOARD: PRAYERS FOR OUR HOME

MATERIALS

White butcher paper to cover the bulletin board
Astrobright paper in a variety of colors
Beige cardstock paper
Scissors
Pushpins
Letter stencils (use die-cutting machine if available)

PREPARATION

- Cover the bulletin board with white cardstock paper
- Use the colored cardstock paper to design a house to go on the bulletin board. Be creative and have fun designing your home!
- Cut the beige cardstock into bricks that are 5″ x 3″ in size. Set these aside.
- Make a plaque that has the key verse printed on it. Add this to the house.

DIRECTIONS

- Give each child a brick and let them write a prayer on it.
- Attach the prayers to the house.

BULLETIN BOARD ILLUSTRATION

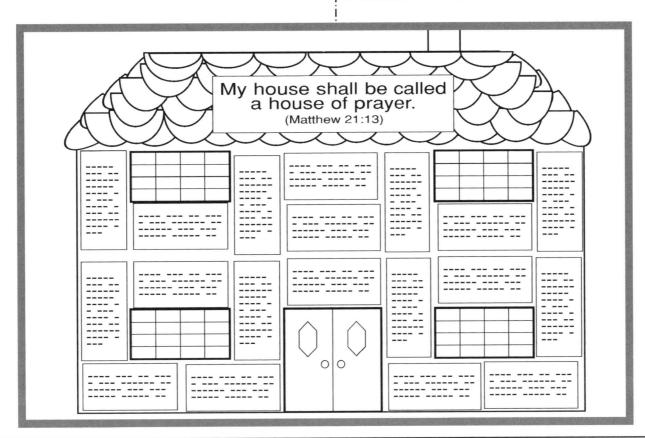

My house shall be called a house of prayer.
(Matthew 21:13)

BONUS PUZZLE: THE LORD'S HOUSE

Use the code below to decipher this message.

A = +
B = !
C = @
D = #
E = $
F = %
G = ^
H = &
I = *
J = (
K =)
L = {
M = }
N = [
O =]
P = \
Q = :
R = ;
S = "
T = '
U = <
V = .
W = ?
X = /
Y = $%
Z = *#

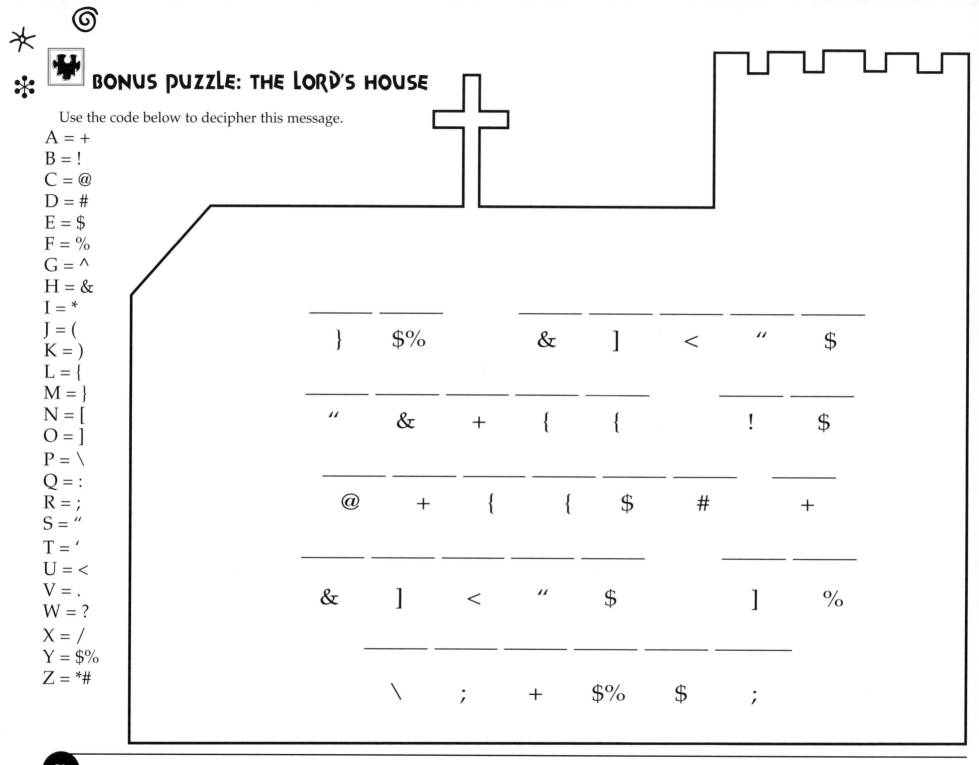

} $%   &] < " $

" & + { {   ! $

@   +   {   { $ #   +

&] < " $] %

\   ;   + $% $;

BONUS PUZZLE SOLUTION:
THE LORD'S HOUSE

Use the code below to decipher this message.

A = +
B = !
C = @
D = #
E = $
F = %
G = ^
H = &
I = *
J = (
K =)
L = {
M = }
N = [
O =]
P = \
Q = :
R = ;
S = "
T = '
U = <
V = .
W = ?
X = /
Y = $%
Z = *#

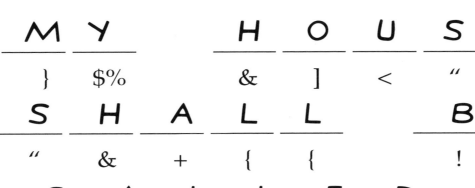

M Y   H O U S E
} $%   &] < " $

S H A L L   B E
" & + { {   ! $

C A L L E D A
@ + { { $ # +

H O U S E   O F
&] < " $] %

P R A Y E R
\ ; + $% $;

DAY 3: TUESDAY—PRAY AND FORGIVE

ROOM SETUP

If possible, use stones to make a large prayer labyrinth in the church-yard. You can also use masking tape to make a large prayer labyrinth in your fellowship hall or another large area in your church building.

SCRIPTURE: MATTHEW 21:18-22; MARK 11:20-25

Key Verse (Mark 11:24): "Whatever you ask for in prayer, believe that you have received it, and it will be yours."

THEME

We need to understand the importance of prayer and forgiveness.

DISCUSSION

Let the kids look at the labyrinth. Explain that this is a prayer labyrinth. Tell the children that a labyrinth is different from a maze. A maze is designed to trick us, mix us up, and get us lost. A labyrinth is designed to lead us to Jesus. It does not trick us, mix us up, or get us lost. While we walk the labyrinth, we pray quietly and think about Jesus. We can pray about whatever we need to pray about.

Talk about why we pray. Let the kids share their thoughts on prayer and what they pray for.

Ask the kids if we get everything we pray for. (*No, of course we don't.*) When we pray for something, it does have to be in God's will to give it to us. When God doesn't give us what we pray for, that doesn't mean God doesn't love us. It means that God has something in mind that is much better for us. We need to have faith in God and trust that the Lord will do what is best for us.

Ask the children if their parents give them *everything* they ask for. (*No, they don't.*) Why don't parents give us everything we ask for? (*We would get spoiled. It's not always good for us. They cannot afford it. They have something better in mind.*)

Talk about the kinds of things we should or should not pray for.

Remind the children that we need to forgive those who have done wrong/bad things to us. Jesus wants us to forgive, even when that's difficult to do.

SOMETHING SPECIAL

Read over both versions of this story, and tell the story in your own words.

SONG

"Oh Hear Our Prayer" (*"Oh When the Saints"*)
> Oh hear our prayer (*clap, clap, clap, clap*)
> This prayer we pray (*clap, clap, clap, clap*)
> Oh hear this prayer we pray to you.
> Oh hear our prayer, Lord Jesus (*clap, clap, clap, clap*)
> Oh hear this prayer we pray to you. (*clap, clap, clap, clap*)
> (*Repeat, with stamping feet.*)

ACTIVITY: WALKING THE LABYRINTH

Let the kids walk the labyrinth.

CREATIVE WRITING ACTIVITY

Help the children compose a group prayer. Write it down. Let children create individual prayers and write them down.

CRAFT: HAND LABYRINTH

Instructions are on page 85.

 ## WORSHIP TIE-IN: KEEP PRAYING!

Ask the children to come to the front of the sanctuary. Have a large poster board with a labyrinth drawn on it. Talk about what a labyrinth is. Read the prayer the children composed as a group, and let them sing the song they learned. After the children have sung the song once, let the congregation join them in singing it. Invite the congregation to walk the prayer labyrinth and also to use the hand labyrinth on the bulletin board after worship.

 ## BULLETIN BOARD: MOVE THROUGH THE LABYRINTH

Instructions are on page 85.

CRAFT: HAND LABYRINTH

MATERIALS
White cardboard circles for pizzas or cakes (found in craft supply stores)
Labyrinth pattern
Pencils
One small bottle of glue per child

PREPARATION
• Make one copy of the labyrinth pattern per child.

DIRECTIONS
• Give each child a labyrinth pattern and a pencil. Tell the children

to turn their labyrinth patterns face down. Have them use their pencils to color the back of the pattern. They should cover the entire page with pencil coloring.
• Give each child a cardboard circle. Have them turn their labyrinth patterns over and place them on top of the circle, so the labyrinth is showing.
• Have them take their pencils and trace over the labyrinth.
• Once the entire pattern is traced, they should remove their patterns. The labyrinth pattern should appear on the circle.
• Give each child a bottle of glue, and tell them to use the glue to draw over the pencil lines of their labyrinth.
• Tell the kids to let these dry for a couple of days. Once they are dry, the kids can "walk" the labyrinth with their fingers. As they "walk" the labyrinth they can think about Jesus and pray.

HAND LABYRINTH PATTERN

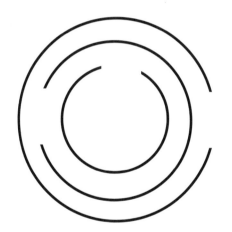

Adjust size as neccesary

 ## BULLETIN BOARD: MOVE THROUGH THE LABYRINTH

Use the pattern on the next page, but make your bulletin board labyrinth larger.

BONUS PUZZLE:
MOVE ON THROUGH

Find your way to Jesus by using your pencil to trace your way through the labyrinth. After you arrive in the middle, turn your paper over, and write a prayer to Jesus.

BONUS PUZZLE SOLUTION: MOVE ON THROUGH

Find your way to Jesus by using your pencil to trace your way through the labyrinth. After you arrive in the middle, turn your paper over, and write a prayer to Jesus.

DAY 4: WEDNESDAY—SHE GAVE IT ALL (WIDOW'S OFFERING)

ROOM SETUP

Have a large box labeled FREEWILL OFFERINGS sitting on a table where the children can easily see it. Have another box labeled TEMPLE TAX sitting next to the freewill offerings box.

Make stained glass "windows" for your room. You'll need a roll of stained glass contact paper and two large empty cardboard picture frames. Cover the frames on both sides with the contact paper. Use book tape to tape the frames together on the back so they will stand upright on the table. Put several votive candles into short glass containers and light them. When finished, you can easily close up the "windows" and store them flat.

SCRIPTURE: MARK 12:41-44; LUKE 21:1-4

Key Verses (Mark 12:43-44): "Truly I tell you, this poor widow has put in more than all those who are contributing to the treasury. For all of them have contributed out of their abundance; but she out of her poverty has put in everything she had, all she had to live on."

THEME

We need to be generous in our giving.

SOMETHING SPECIAL

Read this story aloud:
Mr. Floop's Lunch by Matt Novak

DISCUSSION

Talk about what happened with sharing in the story.

Give each child a different amount of play money in bills (no coins). One of the children will only be given two pennies. Take this child aside and secretly tell him or her to put both pennies in the box when it is time to collect the offering, even though you tell the other kids not to put all their money in. Tell the child not to tell others of your plan.

Sit down with the children and talk to them about what we are learning about holy week. After a few minutes of discussion, tell the children that you are going to collect the offering. Explain that in Bible times, Jewish people were charged a "temple tax." In addition, Jewish people were also expected to give "freewill offerings" to the church. Today, Jewish people still have to pay a fixed amount to belong to a temple. They also have to pay money to attend High Holy Day services. Tell them that in our church, members are allowed to choose how much they will pledge to the church, and we do not charge people to attend worship services, not even on Christmas and Easter, our high holy days.

We encourage people to *tithe*, which means to give one tenth of your income, but we don't require it. Church members make a pledge telling how much they will give each year. This pledge is what our church needs to pay our church staff and to pay to take care of the church building (bills for electricity, phone, and so on).

We also have the opportunity to give extra gifts to the church. These gifts are used for other things like providing food for hungry people or providing medical care for destitute people.

Tell the children they must put their money into the FREEWILL OFFERINGS box. Each child can choose how much of the money to contribute. Tell them not to give all of their money, because they must have money to live on. Have them show how much they are putting into the box. The child with the two pennies will, of course, put both pennies in the box. Ask the children who gave "the most" money, and who gave "the least" money.

Now tell the story of the widow who gave all she had. Explain that a widow is a woman whose husband has died. From what we know, this poor woman did not have any other family members to help her. She was all alone in the world. She did not have any more money. How was she going to pay her own bills? How was she going to eat?

Explain that Jesus does not expect us to go broke giving money to the church. God understands that we have to have money to pay our bills. But God does expect us to sacrifice some things that we don't really need, so we can give money to help poor people obtain what they need.

Ask the children what things we actually need *(shelter, food, clothing, school supplies)*. Ask them what kinds of things we buy that we don't really need *(DVDs, CDs, computer games, designer clothes)*. Encourage children to think of ways they can make sacrifices of things they don't really need to help others have the money to buy things they really need.

Talk about other gifts we can give to others and to God. These can be gifts that do not cost money. Gifts of time, talents, and sharing are important and helpful too. Help the children think of nonmonetary gifts they can give.

 SONG

"**Give to the Lord**" *("Skip to My Lou")*
>Give, give, give to the Lord!
>Give, give, give to the Lord!
>Give, give, give to the Lord!
>Give to the Lord with all your heart.

 ACTIVITY: WE'RE COLLECTING

Instructions are on page 89.

 CRAFT: OFFERING BOXES

Instructions are on page 90.

 WORSHIP TIE-IN: WHAT CAN WE GIVE?

Work with the children to help them decide what kind of special mission they would like to collect money for. They could raise money for an animal shelter, a shelter that helps abused women and children, or an organization that buys school supplies for needy children. Provide them with up to three options. Explain the options to the children and let them vote on it.

Tell the congregation that the children learned the story about the Widow's Offering. Explain that the children have decided to collect a special offering that will benefit the agency they chose. "The children

need our help too. Today while our children's choir sings, some of the other children will pass around the special collection boxes they made. We ask that you donate money to help the children achieve their goal. Each of the children has a box at home where they are collecting money for this agency too."

Use the collection boxes the children designed to collect a special offering from the congregation. Let your children's choir sing the song, "Give to the Lord" while some of the other children pass around the collection boxes during worship. Ask the ushers to guide the children as they pass around the boxes.

 BULLETIN BOARD: THEY NEED OUR HELP

Instructions are on page 90.

 ACTIVITY: WE'RE COLLECTING

MATERIALS
Several shoeboxes with lids
Solid colored wrapping paper or contact paper
Scissors
Magazine photos of pictures that highlight the agency you are collecting for (animals, women and children, school supplies)
Glue sticks
Decoupage solution and brushes

PREPARATION
- Cover the shoeboxes with the wrapping paper or contact paper.
- Wrap the lid and box separately, so the lid can be easily removed.
- Cut a slot in the lid of each box.

DIRECTIONS
- Have the children cut out the magazine photos and glue them to the boxes. If desired, add a layer of decoupage solution.
- These boxes will be used for the Worship Tie-in and then placed by the bulletin board.

CRAFT: OFFERING BOXES

MATERIALS

One small box per child
Decoupage solution
Paintbrushes
Magazine photos
Scissors

PREPARATION

- Cut out lots of magazine photos.
- Cut an opening in the lid of each box.

DIRECTIONS

- Give each child a box.
- Let the children use the decoupage solution to attach the magazine photos to their boxes.
- Tell the children to take the boxes home. They can use them to put in daily coin offerings. Explain that this money will help support the agency they voted on. Encourage the children to think of things they can give up in order to have money for their boxes.
- Have the children bring the boxes to church on Easter Sunday. The money can be given to the agency the children selected.
- Tally all of the money you received from your special offering and from the children's offerings. Let the children know how much money they donated. Tell them that God is very pleased with their generosity.

BULLETIN BOARD: THEY NEED OUR HELP

MATERIALS

Dark blue paper
Bright yellow paper
Scissors
Pushpins
Yarn
School supplies
Letter stencils (use die-cutting machine if available)
Pictures of things that highlight the agency you are collecting for (pets in shelters, women and children, actual school supplies)

PREPARATION

- Cover the board with blue paper.
- Cut out the title THEY NEED OUR HELP from the yellow paper and attach it to the board.

DIRECTIONS

- Attach the pictures or items to the board.

BULLETIN BOARD ILLUSTRATION

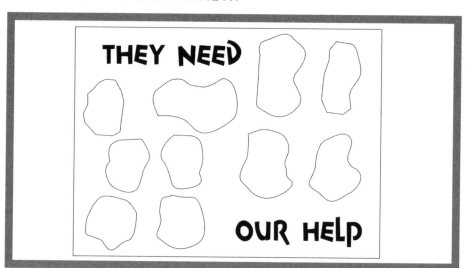

BONUS PUZZLE: WHAT DID SHE GIVE?

Read and answer the clues below. When finished, the circled letters will spell out the answer to the question above. You can find all of the answers if you read both versions of the story in the Bible.

1. The people put their money into the temple ___.

2. The woman in the story was a ___.

3. The woman put in ___ coins.

4. The coins were made of ___.

5. The woman lived in ___.

6. Jesus told this story to the ____.

7. The people made ___ to the temple.

8. ___ is the person who told this story.

1. ◯RE _ S _ RY

2. WIDO◯

3. _W◯

4. ◯_P _ _R

5. P◯V _ R _ Y

6. DISC◯PL _ _

7. _ _ ◯TR_BU_IO_S

8. J _ ◯ _ _

BONUS PUZZLE SOLUTION: WHAT DID SHE GIVE?

Read and answer the clues below. When finished, the circled letters will spell out the answer to the question above. You can find all of the answers if you read both versions of the story in the Bible.

1. The people put their money into the temple ___.

2. The woman in the story was a ___.

3. The woman put in ___ coins.

4. The coins were made of ___.

5. The woman lived in ___.

6. Jesus told this story to the ____.

7. The people made ___ to the temple.

8. ___ is the person who told this story.

1. T R E A S U R Y

2. W I D O W

3. T W O

4. C O P P E R

5. P O V E R T Y

6. D I S C I P L E S

7. C O N T R I B U T I O N S

8. J E S U S

DAY 5: THURSDAY—IN THE GARDEN OF GETHSEMANE

 ## ROOM SETUP

Make the room look like a darkened garden at night. Cover the windows with dark paper. Turn out the room lights. Light the room with votive candles in containers that cannot topple over. Bring in large rocks, containers of artificial flowers, and plants. Find a large mat of green plastic patio covering and place it among the plants, flowers, and rocks. Invite the children to sit in the "garden" with you. Tell the children that this is similar to the garden where Jesus went after celebrating Passover and the Last Supper with his disciples.

 ## SCRIPTURE: MATTHEW 26:36-75; MARK 14:32-72; LUKE 22:39-65

Key Verse (Matthew 26:39): "My Father, if it is possible, let this cup pass from me; yet not what I want but what you want."

 ## THEME

Just as God had a plan for Jesus, God has a plan for us. It's important to follow God's plan even when it's difficult.

 ## SOMETHING SPECIAL

Read and study all three biblical versions of this story. Put the story into your own words and tell it to the children.
—or—
Share either of these stories with the children:

The Cross in the Egg by Shirley Taylor. One of the eggs in the basket has a crack shaped like a cross.

The Rabbit and the Promise Sign by Pat Day-Bivins and Philip Dale Smith. A little rabbit who stays in the Garden of Gethsemane with Jesus receives a very special gift from him.

 ## DISCUSSION

Ask the children if they have ever felt afraid and alone. What's it like to feel that way? Ask if they have ever felt betrayed by their friends. How would you feel if your friends promised to stay with you but then did what the disciples did?

How would you feel if you got in trouble and your best friend did what Peter did to Jesus and said, "I don't know this kid! I've never seen that kid!" Let the children's responses guide your discussion. Explain that Jesus loves us so much that he was willing to die for our sins. Because Jesus died for our sins, we can live with him in heaven after we die.

Some children may share true stories about family members or friends who have died. If they do, reassure them that these people are living happily in heaven with Jesus.

 ## SONG

"Jesus Went into the Garden" *("Mary Had a Little Lamb")*
>Jesus went into the garden, into the garden, into the garden;
>Jesus went into the garden, the Garden of Gethsemane.
>There alone, he prayed to God, prayed to God, prayed to God;
>There alone, he prayed to God to give him strength and courage.

 ## ACTIVITY: A BOUQUET OF LOVE

Instructions are on page 94.

CRAFT: A GARDEN OF LOVE

Instructions are on page 94.

 ## BULLETIN BOARD: GOD'S GARDEN OF LOVE

Instructions are on page 95.

 ## WORSHIP TIE-IN: INTO THE GARDEN

Have a group of people (children, teens, adults) create a pulpit drama of this story. Let the children sing the song, "Jesus Went into the Garden" as part of the drama. Present this to the congregation as part of your Maundy Thursday worship service.

ACTIVITY: A BOUQUET OF LOVE

MATERIALS
Green pipe cleaners
Flower patterns
Black markers
Clear book tape
Large flower vase

PREPARATION
- Use a marker to print a question about Jesus on each flower. Use questions that pertain to the stories the children have studied. (Who was Jesus' mother? Where was Jesus born? How many disciples did Jesus have?) Also include questions about this lesson.
- Use tape to attach each flower to a green pipe cleaner.
- Put the flowers into a vase.

DIRECTIONS
- Have the children sit on the floor with you.
- Let each child select a flower from the vase and read the question.
- See if the child can correctly answer the question. If not, see if anyone else knows the answer. If no one remembers the answer, gently lead the children and help them remember the answer.

 ## CRAFT: A GARDEN OF LOVE

MATERIALS
One small plastic planter per child
Several bags of potting soil
Trowel
Annual flowers that are in bloom
Colored aquarium pebbles
Craft sticks (long and short)
One heavy-duty plastic spoon per child
Glue

PREPARATION
- Fill all of the planters with potting soil.
- Use a hot glue gun to glue one short craft stick across the long craft stick to make a cross. Make one for each child. Let these dry before using.

DIRECTIONS
- Give each child a planter, a plastic spoon, and several flowers. Let them plant the flowers into their planters.
- Have the kids insert the cross into the middle of the planter.
- Give each child some colored pebbles to sprinkle on top of the dirt in their planters.
- Remind children to keep the planter in a sunny location and to water their flowers. The children can keep the flowers in their planters or replant them in their gardens when the weather is warm enough.

BULLETIN BOARD: GOD'S GARDEN OF LOVE

MATERIALS

Blue, green (dark and light), red, yellow, orange, pink, and purple paper
Pushpins
Flower pattern (use die-cutting machine if available)
Colored markers
Letter stencils (use die-cutting machine if available)

PREPARATION

- Cover the top half of the bulletin board with blue paper.
- Cover the bottom half of the bulletin board with green paper cut to look like hills.

- Cut out one flower pattern per child.
- Cut stems and leaves out of the green paper and attach them to the bulletin board. Make the stems different heights.
- Cut out the title GOD'S GARDEN OF LOVE from yellow paper and attach it to the board.

DIRECTIONS

- Give each child a flower pattern and a marker.
- Tell the kids to write how they show their love for Jesus on the flower.
- Attach each child's flower to the board.

BULLETIN BOARD ILLUSTRATION

BONUS PUZZLE: WHAT DID GOD DO?

Use a red pencil or pen to fill in the missing letters in the Bible verse What's the message?

For ___od so
l___ved the
worl___ that He gave
His on___y begotten
S___n
so that e___eryone who
beli___ves in Him
may not peri___h
b___t have
everla___ting life.

BONUS PUZZLE SOLUTION: WHAT DID GOD DO?

Use a red pencil or pen to fill in the missing letters in the Bible verse What's the message?

For _G_od so
l_O_ved the
worl_D_ that He gave
His on_L_y begotten
S_O_n
so that e_V_eryone who
beli_E_ves in Him
may not peri_S_h
b_U_t have
everla_S_ting life.

DAY 6: FRIDAY—CRUCIFY HIM!

ROOM SETUP

Keep the darkened room from day 5. Place a large, wooden, empty cross in one corner of the room. Make another corner of the room look like a tomb by using large pieces of heavy duty cardboard fashioned and painted to look like a tomb. Place a large rock in front of the tomb.

Ask one person in the congregation to dress as Mary, the mother of Jesus, and several people to dress as the disciples. Let them be sitting solemnly next to the tomb when you enter. They will not speak.

SCRIPTURE: MATTHEW 27:32-37; MARK 15:21-24; LUKE 23:26-46; JOHN 19:17

Key Verse (Luke 23:46): "Father, into your hands I commend my spirit."

THEME

Jesus died on the cross to save us from our sins.

SOMETHING SPECIAL

Use a very serious, quiet voice to tell what happened to Jesus when he died on the cross. Tell the events as though you were there to witness them. Use your judgment as to how much detail you want to go into with the children. Talk about how sad Jesus' mother and the disciples were.

Ask the children to share their thoughts on the crucifixion of Jesus. Explain that when Jesus lived, those who had done something really wrong were sometimes crucified on a cross. Many people did not understand that Jesus was a good person who truly wanted to help people. He taught them things and told them things that they had never heard before. The things Jesus said and did frightened some of the people, and they decided that he was wrong to say and do those things. They saw what Jesus did as breaking Jewish law. They just didn't understand. Because they didn't understand, some of them decided they had to kill Jesus, and they did.

Jesus knew that he had to die on the cross to save us from our sins. That was why Jesus was sent to earth. He came to earth to teach us how to live according to God's laws, and then he had to pay for all of our sins by dying. Because Jesus died on the cross, we will go to heaven to live with God when we die. While Jesus was on the cross he asked God to forgive the people who were crucifying him, because they did not know what they were doing.

SONG

"Jesus" (*"Brahm's Lullaby"*)
> Jesus died for our sins
> because he loves us.
> He wants us to be free
> and to live again with God.
> Oh Lord, we love you.
> We'll love you always.
> Be with us, be our guide.
> Oh how we love you.

ACTIVITY: PRAYERS FOR JESUS

Instructions are on page 99.

CRAFT: STAINED GLASS WINDOWS

Instructions are on page 99.

BULLETIN BOARD: PRAYERS FOR JESUS

Instructions are on page 100.

WORSHIP TIE-IN: THEN, WHAT HAPPENED?

Let the children come to the front of the church during the Good Friday service. Read the story *A Child's Easter* by Patricia A. Pingry. Remind the children that, unlike the people back in Jesus' time, we know how the story really ends. We know that Jesus rose from the dead and that he came to save us from our sins. Invite the children to sing "Jesus."

ACTIVITY: PRAYERS FOR JESUS

MATERIALS

One large sheet of heavy-duty black paper
Scissors
Silver gel pens
Pencils

PREPARATION

- Draw a large cross on the black paper. Cut it out. Lay it flat on a table.

DIRECTIONS

- Let the children use the silver gel pens to write prayers for Jesus on the cross. They can sign their names.
- Display the cross in the narthex.

CRAFT: STAINED GLASS WINDOWS

MATERIALS

Waxed paper
Paper clips
Scraps of brightly colored tissue paper

Black paper
Iron and ironing surface
Two large towels
Disposable paper bowls
Tape
One 8" x 10" piece of black paper per child
One glue stick per child

PREPARATION

- Cut out two 8" x 10" pieces of waxed paper per child. Paper clip them together.
- Put the scraps of colored tissue paper into paper bowls.
- Heat the iron.
- Lay the towel on your ironing surface.
- Cut one cross per child from the black paper. (See pattern above.)
- Cut out the center of each 8" x 10" black piece of paper.

DIRECTIONS

- Give each child one piece of the waxed paper.
- Tell them to use a small piece of tape to attach the cross to the waxed paper.
- Let the children arrange the colored tissue squares, so they surround the cross. The colored scraps can go right up to the edges of the cross, but they should not cover any part of the cross.
- Have each child carefully bring the paper over to the ironing area. Set it on top of the towel. Gently lay the second piece of waxed paper on top of the bottom piece. Cover that with the second cloth towel, and press the iron firmly over the towel. This will seal the pieces of waxed paper together.
- Glue the waxed paper over the opening of the black paper, so the black paper makes a frame around the stained glass window.
- Let the children take the crosses home to become part of their Good Friday decorations.

BULLETIN BOARD: PRAYERS FOR JESUS

MATERIALS

Blue paper
Pushpins
Letter stencils (use die-cutting machine if available)
Black paper
Black cardstock paper
Colored thin-tip markers
Silver gel pens

BULLETIN BOARD ILLUSTRATION

PREPARATION

- Cover the board with blue paper.
- Cut out the title from the black cardstock paper and attach it to the board.
- Make a large cross from the black paper.

DIRECTIONS

- Let the kids sign their names to the black cross.
- Attach the cross to the center of the bulletin board.

BONUS PUZZLE SOLUTION: WHO DO I LOVE?

Color: 1=Yellow, 2=Orange, 3=Pink, 4=Red, 5=Green, 6=Blue

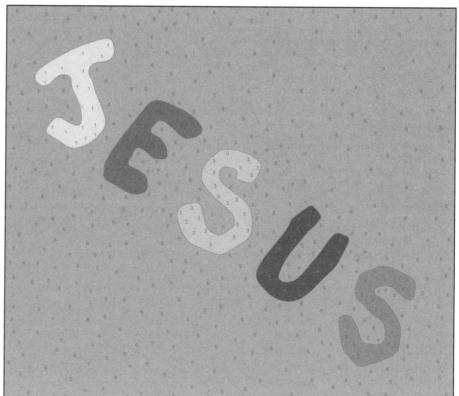

BONUS PUZZLE: WHO DO i LOVE?

Color: 1=Yellow, 2=Orange, 3=Pink, 4=Red, 5=Green, 6=Blue

DAY 7: SUNDAY—CHRIST IS RISEN!

SONSATIONAL SUNDAY CELEBRATION

Present this on the Saturday before Easter or on Easter Sunday. Invite the parents to attend with their children. If possible, combine kindergarten through fifth grade and have a *Sonsational* Sunday Celebration, where families can spend time together.

Set up your fellowship hall, so you can take a Reflection Walk through holy week. Provide a large area rug where the children can sit for the Gathering Time. Surround this with chairs for parents.

You'll have six Stopping Points that go along the walls of your room. Each Stopping Point will feature one of the days of holy week: Sunday—It's a Parade! Monday—Get Out! Tuesday—Pray and Forgive, Wednesday—She Gave It All, Thursday—In the Garden of Gethsemane, Friday—Crucify Him! and Sunday—Christ Is Risen! The seventh Stopping Point, "Sunday—Christ Is Risen!" will be in the Gathering Place.

Each Stopping Point will highlight what happened on that day and feature a related activity for children and parents. Two teachers, dressed in Bible costumes (see p. xii) will be needed to set up and supervise the activities for each Stopping Point. They will portray the townsmen and women. The townsmen and women will also give out the remembrances.

You'll need one berry basket for each child. Make a handle for each basket by attaching two long, sturdy pipe cleaners to it. Put a small amount of green Easter grass in each basket. Provide inexpensive remembrances at each Stopping Point. Children can carry the remembrances in their baskets. At some Stopping Points, the children will create their souvenirs. Parents and children will walk together and participate in the activities at each Stopping Point as they recall the final week of Jesus' life on earth.

The Gathering Place should be the focal point. Use your imagination and make it as colorful as possible. Things such as a large white cross, lots of colorful flowers, banners, streamers, and Mylar balloons will make the area a bright, eye-catching display to honor our risen Lord. Off

to the side, have a tomb with the stone rolled away. Lay some cloth on the ground.

Decorate the room with artwork done by the children during the past six weeks, putting the appropriate artwork by each Stopping Point. See pages 103-105 for instructions on how to set up each Stopping Point.

If you do this on Saturday, let parents and children know this is a "casual and comfy" dress day. If you do it on Easter, expect everyone to be dressed up, so provide smocks or other protective wear to slip over clothing as needed.

Begin the program in the Gathering Place. Children will sit on the rug, and adults will sit in the chairs. Have the room darkened when everyone arrives.

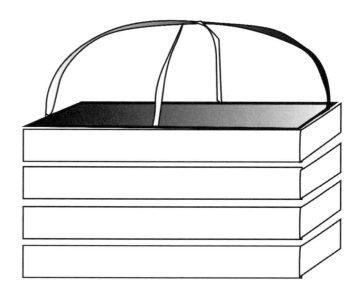

 SCRIPTURE: MATTHEW 28:1-7; MARK 16:1-8; LUKE 24:1-12; JOHN 20:1-10

Key Verse (Luke 24:5): "Why do you look for the living among the dead? He is not here, but has risen."

SOMETHING SPECIAL

Read and study all four Gospel versions of the Resurrection story. Write a short dramatization based on all four versions of the story.

Have several women portray the women who came to the tomb to anoint Jesus. Let them walk quietly into the darkened room and approach the tomb. Have someone else dressed as an angel sit by the tomb. The actors can present a dramatization of the story. The women can discuss the horrible events of Friday when Jesus was crucified. They can say that it is now time to anoint the body of Jesus as was done according to Jewish custom. If you have dimming switches in your room, use them to control the lighting. As the story unfolds, gradually bring up the lights in the room. Hold the room at half-light until the angel says, "Why do you look for the living among the dead? He is not here, but has risen." Then suddenly bring the lights all the way up. If you do not have dimming switches, keep the room dark until the angel makes the announcement. Then turn on the lights.

Have another adult portray Jesus, who can then enter the scene and play out the rest of the story.

Leader: CHRIST IS RISEN!

All Respond: CHRIST IS RISEN INDEED!

Explain that everyone will take a Reflection Walk through the events of holy week. There are seven Stopping Points, one for each day. Each family will travel together. You'll stop at each Stopping Point, where you will participate in the activity there. Children will create or be given a remembrance to put into their baskets. People can travel to the Stopping Points in any order.

Give each child a basket to carry.

BULLETIN BOARD: CHRIST IS RISEN INDEED!

See instructions on page 105.

DAY 1: SUNDAY—IT'S A PARADE!

Set up the area with palm branches strewn about the floor. Have a table set up where children and parents can make palm crosses. You'll need two palm fronds per person and several staplers filled with staples. Give each person one long and one short palm frond. Let them staple the fronds together to make a cross. The cross is the remembrance for this Stopping Point.

Talk about what happened on Palm Sunday. See pages 74-76 for discussion ideas. Remind everyone that the theme of this lesson was "We need to prepare a way for the Lord." How did the people prepare for the arrival of Jesus on that day?

Have the book *The Colt and the King* by Marni McGee on display.

DAY 2: MONDAY—GET OUT! (JESUS CLEARS THE TEMPLE)

Have an overturned table and chairs. Scatter debris from the marketplace on the floor. The teachers can tell what they "witnessed" that day in the temple. Remind children that we have to keep God's house holy. How can we help keep God's house holy? See pages 79-80 for discussion information.

Have a batch of balloons with slips of paper inside them. On each slip will be a word from the Bible verse for this day (Matthew 21:13). Let each child pop a balloon and find the word. Let the kids try to put the words into the correct order so they can read the verse.

Give each child a key ring with the Bible verse attached for a remembrance. You can add a small key if desired (found in hardware and home stores). Tell them this is the key to God's house.

DAY 3: TUESDAY—PRAY AND FORGIVE

Set up a small stone labyrinth on top of the table. Make the labyrinth by hot gluing some small stones to a piece of colored foam core (see pattern p. 86). Let people use their fingers to "walk" through the labyrinth as they pray and forgive. The teachers should talk about the importance of prayer and forgiveness. Give each child a labyrinth puzzle with the tiny silver balls as the remembrance. See pages 84-85 for discussion hints.

Day 4: Wednesday—She Gave it All (Widow's Offering)

Set the stained glass windows and candles on a table. Also set out the offering boxes (p. 90). Have one of the teachers dress as and portray the poor widow. She should be dressed in black scraggly clothing. She can sit on a large pillow on the floor by the windows and the candle. The widow can tell everyone how she gave everything she had to the temple. Discuss how we can give offerings to the Lord. This is where children can leave their Easter offerings. Give each child two play-money coins for the remembrance. See pages 88-89 for discussion ideas.

Day 5: Thursday—In the Garden of Gethsemane

Create a garden in this area (p. 93). Let everyone come into the garden and have a seat on the grass. Talk about what happened to Jesus in the garden. Why do you think Jesus spent time praying in a garden? The garden reminds us that there is always new life. Jesus would give us new life when he rose from the dead. Provide protective smocks here. Have one small plastic pot per person, dirt, small trowels, and some annual flowers. Let everyone scoop dirt into their pots and plant a flower. The potted flowers will be the remembrance at this Stopping Point. See page 93 for discussion ideas.

Day 6: Friday—Crucify Him!

Have three large crosses propped against the wall. Put a piece of artificial green grass and some rocks on the floor. Parents and kids can sit on the grass and rocks. The teachers can dress as and portray those who

crucified Jesus. Let them reenact what happened that day. Have pieces of colored cardstock paper folded in half, to be made into cards. Provide crayons, markers, and a variety of religious stickers. Let each child make a card for Jesus telling how much they love him. Give each child a cross necklace as a remembrance. See page 98 for discussion ideas.

Day 7: Sunday—Christ is Risen!

This will be the last Stopping Point for everyone. Have everyone return to the Gathering Place, where you will share stories and songs. Have one Mylar balloon per child. The balloon will be the remembrance for this Stopping Point.

 ## Something Special

Read this story aloud:
The Easter Story by Carol Heyer

 ## Song

"Christ Is Risen Today! Alleluia!" ("She'll Be Coming 'Round the Mountain")

> Christ is risen today! ALLELUIA!
> Christ is risen today! ALLELUIA!
> Christ is risen! Christ is risen! Christ is risen! Christ is risen!
> Christ is risen today! ALLELUIA!

Give each person a handful of shiny confetti. Sing this song and shout out the Alleluia! Let everyone toss out the confetti. Remind them to take turns tossing the confetti, so that it is being tossed all during the song.

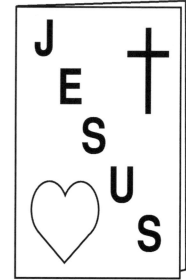

WORSHIP TIE-IN: JESUS IS ALIVE!

Invite the children to come to the front of the church. Read these three short stories to them from the book *He Is Alive!* by Helen Haidle: "Resurrection Morning," "Is It Really True?" and "Surprising Appearances." They tell the story of Jesus' resurrection.

Print the words to "Christ Is Risen Today, Alleluia!" (p. 104) in the bulletin and invite everyone to sing. As they sing, the children can hold their balloons and toss out confetti.

BULLETIN BOARD: CHRIST IS RISEN INDEED!

MATERIALS

White butcher paper
Orange, yellow, and red tempera paints
Paintbrushes
Different shades of yellow astrobright paper
Pushpins
Large white poster board
Gold glitter
Glue

DIRECTIONS

- Water down the orange, red, and yellow tempera paints.
- Use them to paint a sunrise on the white butcher paper. Let it dry. Attach it to the board.
- Cut out a large cross from the white poster board. Cover it with glue and sprinkle it with gold glitter. Let it dry.
- Cut out a half sun from the bright yellow paper.
- Cut out rays of sun from the different shades of the yellow paper.
- Attach the yellow sun and rays to the board.
- When the cross is dry, attach it to the board.

BULLETIN BOARD ILLUSTRATION

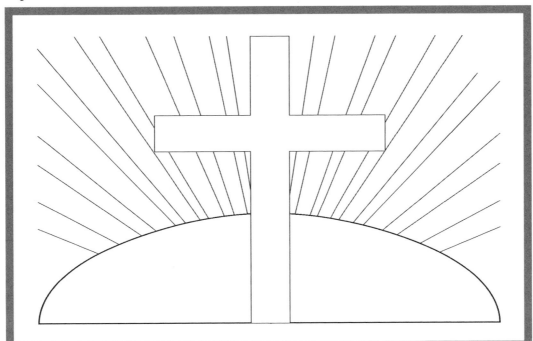

BONUS PUZZLE: WHAT'S GOIN' ON?

Use a yellow marker to draw lines through the words you find in the puzzle. When you are finished you will have a special message. Write the message on the line below.

_____

How many doves did you find in the puzzle? _____

The doves remind us of the Trinity, which is God the _____, Jesus the _____ of God, and the _____ _____ of the Lord.

Jesus	Son	Love
Pray	Crucified	Teach
Widow	Palm	Forgives Us
Helps	Temple	You
Friend	Miracles	Go
Resurrection	Garden	Cross
Savior	God	Sins
Me	Oh	Cares

C	H	R	I	S	T	M	L	H	C	R	F
J	W	I	D	O	W	E	O	E	R	E	R
E	P	R	A	Y	🕊	I	V	L	O	S	I
S	T	S	I	N	S	S	E	P	S	U	E
U	E	G	A	R	D	E	N	S	S	R	N
S	A	V	I	O	R	P	A	L	M	R	D
O	C	Y	O	U	R	I	S	E	N	E	C
H	H	T	E	M	P	L	E	🕊	S	C	A
C	R	U	C	I	F	I	E	D	O	T	R
G	O	D	I	N	D	E	E	D	N	I	E
F	O	R	G	I	V	E	S	U	S	O	S
M	I	R	A	C	L	E	S	G	O	N	🕊

Use a yellow marker to draw lines through the words you find in the puzzle. When you are finished you will have a special message. Write the message on the line below.

CHRIST IS RISEN INDEED

How many doves did you find in the puzzle? **3**

The doves remind us of the Trinity, which is God the **CREATOR**, Jesus the **SON** of God, and the **HOLY** **SPIRIT** of the Lord.

Jesus	Son	Love
Pray	Crucified	Teach
Widow	Palm	Forgives Us
Helps	Temple	You
Friend	Miracles	Go
Resurrection	Garden	Cross
Savior	God	Sins
Me	Oh	Cares

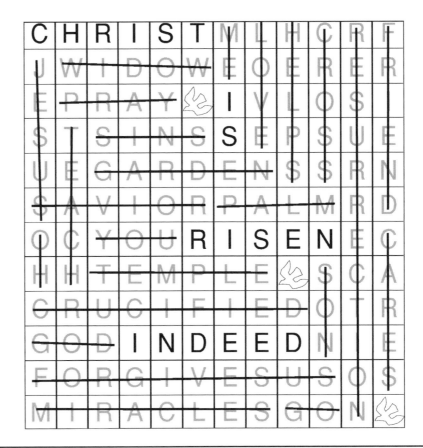

Section Four

ALL YEAR LONG

This section includes entertaining group activities that can be enjoyed throughout the year by all members of your church family. Intergenerational events allow children, youth, and adults the joy of interacting with people of all ages.

There is one social activity suggested for each month. Let these be evangelism opportunities, and invite visitors. Publicize these activities in your local newspapers, with posters, and by distributing flyers in the area surrounding your church. Ask church members to distribute informative flyers in their neighborhoods. Encourage members to bring friends and neighbors to your happenings.

Conclude each social event with a brief time of prayer and singing, and invite visitors to attend worship services and Christian education classes. Try to get names, addresses, and phone numbers of visitors so your evangelism team can contact them.

Consider giving a small gift to each visitor (Christian activity book for children, small devotional booklet for adults) the first time they visit your church. Provide information about your church and its programs as well.

There is also a service project for each month of the year. When people are involved in ongoing service projects, they begin to appreciate the blessings they have, and they learn to share with those less fortunate. Invite all church members to take part in these activities so they become church family events.

You will also find a bulletin board for each month. Put this bulletin board in a prominent place in your church so that many people have the opportunity to see it. Set up an area where you can display information about forthcoming programs. Allow a place for people to register for upcoming events.

Now begin planning some awesome activities, remembering whenever two or more are gathered in God's name, God is there with you.

IMPORTANT REMINDERS

- When you take children off church property for activities, get a permission slip signed by the child's parents or guardians. Make sure children have health forms on file that list health problems (for example, diabetes, allergies) that children may have. Request that parents sign a slip allowing you to get treatment for their children in case of unexpected illness or injury. Keep these with you at all times. Take a list of the children's names, birth dates, home phone numbers, cell phone numbers, and a phone number where parents can be reached in case of an emergency. All adults should carry a fully charged cell phone when taking children off church property.
- Have each child wear a name tag that includes the child's first and last name as well as the church name, address, and phone number to serve as identification should a child become separated from the group.
- Have two adults (or one adult and one high school student) per group of five to six children to allow for adequate supervision. Review the rules of staying side-by-side with the adults, not wandering off, and not talking to strangers. Those supervising children should *always* be able to see the children. Children should remain within *touching distance* of supervisors at all times. Children should *never* be left unattended or allowed to wander off on their own.
- When children remain on church property, make sure parents leave a phone number where they can be reached in case of an emergency.
- Develop a "behavior code" for all who participate in your programs. This should define both acceptable and unacceptable behaviors. Children and parents or guardians should sign it. Let all know the consequences of misbehavior.

JANUARY

KEY SCRIPTURE VERSE

Matthew 18:20: "For where two or three are gathered in my name, I am there among them."

MOVIE MADNESS

Invite all members of your congregation to enjoy an afternoon or an evening of "Movie Madness." Advertise this event in your local newspaper and invite members of the community to attend. Design an advertising display to put outside your church so that people driving by can see it.

Set up a ticket booth and concession stand. Use the money collected from the ticket fees and concession stand to support your church's evangelism program. Provide attractive, informative flyers about your church to distribute.

You'll need several TVs and VCRs or DVD players. Ask families to bring videos and DVDs, or stop by your local public library or a video store to rent movies that are suitable for family viewing. Let people decide which film to attend. All films should run approximately the length of time. At the end of the movies, invite everyone to the sanctuary for a brief sing-along of joyful Christian songs and a time of prayer.

JANUARY SERVICE PROJECT: MOVIES FOR YOU!

Ask each family or individual to donate gently used videos or DVDs they no longer use. Donate these to a nursing home.

JANUARY BULLETIN BOARD: IT'S SNOW MUCH BETTER TO PRAY TOGETHER

MATERIALS
Blue fadeless paper
Letter stencils (use die-cutting machine if available)
White batting
White, red, green, yellow, black, orange, and purple cardstock paper
Pushpins
Glue
Scissors
Pencils

DIRECTIONS
- Cover the bulletin board with blue fadeless paper.
- Attach white batting to look like snow.
- Cut out snowflakes from white cardstock paper. Attach them to the board.
- Make one large snowman and several smaller snow people out of white cardstock paper.
- Cut out black circles for the eyes and mouths. Cut out orange carrot noses. Glue the eyes, noses, and mouths to the snow people.
- Cut out hats from the colored paper and glue them on.
- Attach the snow people to the board.
- Use the white paper to make arms for each snow person. Use the black paper to make mittens for each snow person. Glue the mittens to the hands and attach the arms to each snow person. Glue the hands together, so it looks like the snow people are praying.
- Use letter stencils to make the title IT'S *SNOW* MUCH BETTER TO PRAY TOGETHER from white paper. Attach the title to the board.

IT'S SNOW MUCH BETTER TO PRAY TOGETHER

FEBRUARY

KEY SCRIPTURE VERSE

Psalm 117:2: "For great is his steadfast love toward us, and the faithfulness of the LORD endures forever."

VALENTINE'S DINNER

Host a Valentine's Dinner where everything you serve is heart-shaped as well as red or pink. See how creative people can be in designing a variety of heart-shaped red and pink foods.

Play the game "God's Heart." Use an electronic concordance to find Bible verses that speak of love. Cut out large hearts from red and pink paper. Use a black marker to print one Bible verse on each heart. Laminate the hearts. Cut them in half. Put all of the hearts into a Valentine gift bag. Let each person reach inside the bag and select half a heart. Participants must find the person who matches their heart. Have each group of two participants spend some time getting to know each other.

Spend time talking about how God shows love for us. Sing songs that speak of God's love. Visit your local public library to find stories about Valentine's Day, friendship, and love. Ask members of your congregation to read these aloud.

FEBRUARY SERVICE PROJECT: LOVELY LOCKS

Team up with local beauty salons in your area to sponsor a "Locks of Love" Drive. People with long hair can donate their hair to be used to make hairpieces for children who have lost their hair due to chemotherapy treatments or other illnesses. Visit www.locksoflove.org for additional information. Read the book *Hattie, Get a Haircut!* by Jenna Glatzer to help people learn about this wonderful service.

FEBRUARY BULLETIN BOARD: Let's Talk Love

MATERIALS

Black construction paper
Colored construction paper
Scissors
Black thin-tipped felt markers
Pushpins

DIRECTIONS

- Cover the bulletin board with black paper.
- Cut out heart shapes from different colors of construction paper.
- Have each person print a message of love on a heart, using a black marker, and attach it to the board. These can be Bible verses that speak of love or individual thoughts about love.

MARCH

KEY SCRIPTURE VERSE

Psalm 9:2: "I will be glad and exult in you;
I will sing praise to your name, O Most High."

HYMN SING

Host a Hymn Sing at your church. Work with your Music Director to choose a wide variety of hymns that will appeal to all ages. Introduce people to some new songs. Choose some songs that allow for movement and expression. Be creative in how you present the songs. Take a freewill offering that will benefit your children's music program.

MARCH SERVICE PROJECT: SKATE ON!

Gather church members for a night of roller-skating at a local skate rink. Let members pledge a certain amount of money for each 15-minute skating segment. The money raised can be donated to "Wheels for the World," an organization that refurbishes and provides wheelchairs to needy individuals around the world. Visit www.joniandfriends.org for additional information about this organization.

MARCH BULLETIN BOARD: SING A SONG OF GOD'S LOVE

MATERIALS

Music paper for the background (in scrapbooking stores)
Black musical notes
Red cardstock paper
Letter stencils (use die-cutting machine if available)
Scissors
White self-stick labels (1" x 2 5/8")
Red, thin, felt-tipped markers
Pushpins

PREPARATION

- Cover the bulletin board with the music paper.
- Cut out the title from the red paper and attach it to the board.

DIRECTIONS

- Give each person a white label and instruct them to use the red markers to print the title of their favorite hymn or Christian song on it.
- Stick each label to a black musical note and attach the notes to the bulletin board.

PATTERNS FOR NOTES

APRIL

KEY SCRIPTURE VERSE

Zechariah 3:5: "And I said, 'Let them put a clean turban on his head.' So they put a clean turban on his head and clothed him with the apparel; and the angel of the LORD was standing by."

IN YOUR EASTER BONNET

Invite kids to church to create their own special Easter bonnets.

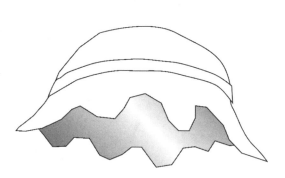

MATERIALS
Large, 20" + -square sheets
   of sturdy white paper
One 6"-diameter bowl
Glue sticks
Masking tape
Crepe paper streamers
Ribbons
Scissors
6" or larger rubber bands
Stickers
Self-stick foam shapes

PREPARATION
- Mold the paper over the bowl to make a hat for each child.
- Secure the paper with one of the rubber bands.
- Run tape around the base of the hat twice to hold it in place.
- Remove the rubber band and take the hat off the bowl.

DIRECTIONS
- Give each child a hat to decorate using streamers, ribbons, stickers, and self-stick foam shapes. Trim the edges.

Let the kids wear their hats and have an Easter Hat Parade. Tell the children we often adorn ourselves with new clothes at Easter in honor of the resurrected Jesus. In Bible times people wore head coverings to show respect for the Lord.

APRIL SERVICE PROJECT: BUNNIES, BOOKS, 'N' BASKETS

Purchase Easter baskets and fill them with a stuffed bunny, an Easter activity and coloring book, chocolate bunnies, eggs, jellybeans, and an Easter storybook. Donate these to needy children in your community or to church children who are homebound or hospitalized.

APRIL BULLETIN BOARD: A BASKET OF EASTER BLESSINGS

MATERIALS
Yellow paper to cover the board
Different shades of brown paper
Letter stencils (use a die-cutting machine if available)
Pushpins
Colored astrobright paper (green, red, pink, orange, purple, blue)
Green Easter grass

PREPARATION
- Cover the board with yellow paper.
- Cut out the title from orange paper and attach it to the board.
- Use the brown paper to make a woven basket. Attach the basket to the board.
- Cut egg shapes out of the colored paper.

DIRECTIONS
- Give each person a colored egg and a marker. Tell them to write a blessing on the egg.
- Attach the eggs to the board.

A Basket of Easter Blessings

FRIENDS

JESUS

LOVE

FAMILY

MY HAMSTER

TOYS

FOOD

MAY

KEY SCRIPTURE VERSE

Proverbs 9:9: "Give instruction to the wise, and they will become wiser still; teach the righteous and they will gain in learning."

FUNDAY

Choose a Saturday or Sunday afternoon to host a preview of your summer vacation Bible school and summer Sunday school programs. Set up different activity centers (art, music, puppets, creative dramatics, cooking). Ask the adults who will be working with VBS and summer Sunday school to host these centers.

Begin with a brief worship time, where you sing, pray, and share a story. See my book, *Worship Time with Kids*, for ideas. Let the children visit the activity centers to preview vacation Bible school and summer Sunday school activities. Give each child a coupon for a prize that can be redeemed at vacation Bible school or Sunday school.

MAY SERVICE PROJECT: DONATIONS!

Ask church members to donate items that you will need for VBS and summer Sunday school.

MAY BULLETIN BOARD: LOOK WHAT'S COMIN' UP!

MATERIALS

Yellow paper to cover the board
Bright colored cardstock paper
Letter stencils (use a die-cutting machine if available)

Pushpins
Information about vacation Bible school and summer Sunday school

DIRECTIONS

- Cover the board with the yellow paper.
- Cut out and attach the title from any color paper.
- Add pictures and information about vacation Bible school and summer Sunday school.

PRIZE COUPON
GOOD FOR ONE
FREE PRIZE
AT VBS

JUNE

KEY SCRIPTURE VERSE

Deuteronomy 4:29: "From there you will seek the LORD your God, and you will find him if you search after him with all your heart and soul."

"SEEK AND YOU SHALL FIND" ROAD RALLY

Do this on a Saturday or Sunday afternoon when there is plenty of daylight. Ask people to bring instant cameras loaded with film. Determine ahead of time how many exposures you want on the roll of film and have people bring the same thing. You could also provide these for people. Develop a list of things you want people to photograph. Be creative in designing your lists and make it interesting by varying each list. Each list should have some of the same items as well as a few items that are different. Include things having to do with: church, God and religion (churches of a different denomination, things God created, crosses), school, a library, and a fast-food place. Divide people into teams who will travel by car or van to find and photograph the items on the list. Give people two to three hours to find and photograph the items listed. The team with the most correct photographs wins the event. Provide fun prizes for the winning team. Have a cookout with hotdogs, hamburgers, chips, beverages, and ice-cream cones when people return.

JUNE SERVICE PROJECT: JUST FOR DADS

Ask all members of the congregation to donate items that can be used by dads of new babies.

JUNE BULLETIN BOARD: FAMOUS BIBLE DADS

MATERIALS

Pictures of famous Bible dads and their children (look in Bible storybooks)
Yellow paper
Pushpins
Letter stencils (use a die-cutting machine if available)
Labels with the names of the dads and kids
Yarn

PREPARATION

- Cover the board with yellow paper.
- Cut out the title and attach it to the board.
- Cut out the pictures of the dads and kids. Attach the dads to the left side of the board. Put their names under their pictures. Attach the kids to the right side of the board. Put their names under their pictures.
- Do not put the kids directly across from their own dads. Attach a long strand of yarn next to each dad.

DIRECTIONS

- Let people try to guess which dad is the father of which child. They can connect the yarn from the dads to the kids.

FAMOUS BIBLE DADS

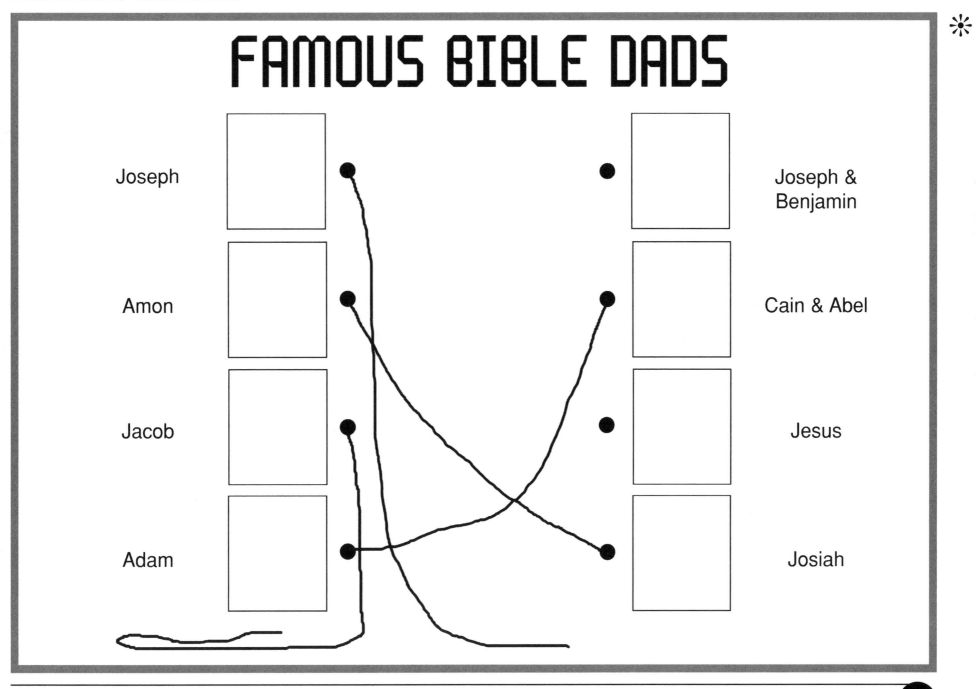

Joseph

Amon

Jacob

Adam

Joseph & Benjamin

Cain & Abel

Jesus

Josiah

JULY

KEY SCRIPTURE VERSE

2 Corinthians 3:17: "Now the Lord is the Spirit, and where the Spirit of the Lord is, there is freedom."

PARK-N-PARTY

Plan a Fourth of July party to take place in your church parking lot. Provide food, game booths, storytelling, music, crafts, and more. Advertise this with posters, articles in your local newspaper, and signs in front of your church. Distribute flyers to the neighbors surrounding your church and ask members to distribute flyers in their neighborhoods. Invite guests to attend your church and give them informative flyers about your programs.

JULY SERVICE PROJECT: JUST FOR YOU!

Donate money or put together kits of supplies to be sent to men and women in our armed services. Contact a nearby military installation to assist you with the logistics of sending your materials to military personnel abroad.

JULY BULLETIN BOARD: FREE TO PRAY

MATERIALS
White paper to cover the board
Small, hand-held American flags on sticks
Shiny red paper
Letter stencils (use a die-cutting machine if available)
Pushpins
Blue felt markers

PREPARATION
- Cover the board with white paper.
- Cut the title out of red paper and attach it to the board.
- Attach the flags around the outer edges of the board.

DIRECTIONS
- Let people use the blue markers to write prayers for our country on the white paper.

LOVE EACH OTHER

THE CHILDREN

THE PRESIDENT OF THE U.S.A.!

OUR TROOPS!

FREE TO PRAY

TO END ALL FIGHTING!

SAFETY!

EVERYONE GET ALONG!

STAY STRONG!

PEACE!

AUGUST

KEY SCRIPTURE VERSE

Psalm 119:73: "Your hands have made and fashioned me;
give me understanding that I may learn your commandments."

EXTREME WEEK

Plan a week filled with activities. Do something different each day of the week beginning with Sunday and ending on Saturday. Visit an amusement park, a water park, a museum, a zoo; see a movie; attend a play or concert; go to the beach, and so on. Take the Lord with you and praise God's name at every venue. Celebrate the last of summer vacation, as school will be starting soon!

AUGUST SERVICE PROJECT: I'VE GOT SHOES!

Ask members to donate a new pair of children's or teen's gym shoes. Give these to a local school so needy children have a pair of gym shoes to keep at school for physical education classes.

AUGUST BULLETIN BOARD: TAKE JESUS TO SCHOOL

MATERIALS

White paper large enough to cover the board
Large picture of a school (found in teacher supply stores)
Large picture of Jesus
Pushpins
Red cardstock paper
Letter stencils (use a die-cutting machine if available)
Brightly colored markers (red, blue, green, purple)

PREPARATION

- Cover the board with white paper.
- Attach the school and picture of Jesus to the board.
- Cut the title out of red paper and attach it to the board.

DIRECTIONS

- Invite people to write prayers for the coming school year on the white paper.

Take Jesus

STUDENTS

BE HONEST

BE KIND TO ALL

LEARN ALL YOU CAN

REMEMBER GOD LOVES YOU

TEACHERS

OBEY THE RULES

to School

SEPTEMBER

KEY SCRIPTURE VERSE

Proverbs 22:6: "Train children in the right way, and when old, they will not stray."

FANTASTIC FAMILY FUN NIGHTS

Begin a series of monthly "Fantastic Family Fun Nights" on Friday nights. Kids and parents *must* attend together. Choose a theme for each month. Share stories, songs, games, puppet shows, snacks, and crafts that relate to each month's theme. Have activities for all ages. See my books *Bible Banquets with Kids* and *Bible Verse Fun with Kids* for ideas.

SEPTEMBER SERVICE PROJECT: SCHOOL SUPPLIES

Have church members donate school supplies (pencils, color pencils, pens, markers, paper). Give these to the local homeless shelter so children using the shelter have supplies to help them do their schoolwork.

SEPTEMBER BULLETIN BOARD: BACK TO SUNDAY SCHOOL

MATERIALS

Yellow paper to cover the board
Bright green cardstock paper
Letter stencils (use a die-cutting machine if available)
Pushpins
Pictures highlighting what you'll be doing in Sunday school
Thin felt-tip markers

PREPARATION

- Cover the board with yellow paper.
- Cut out the title from green cardstock and attach it to the board.
- Attach the pictures highlighting your upcoming program.

DIRECTIONS

- Let the kids use the markers to sign their names on the board.

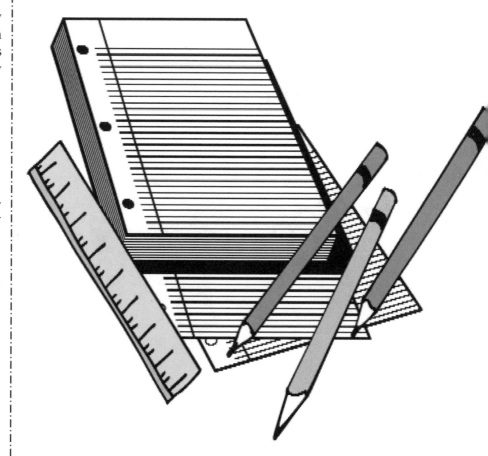

126

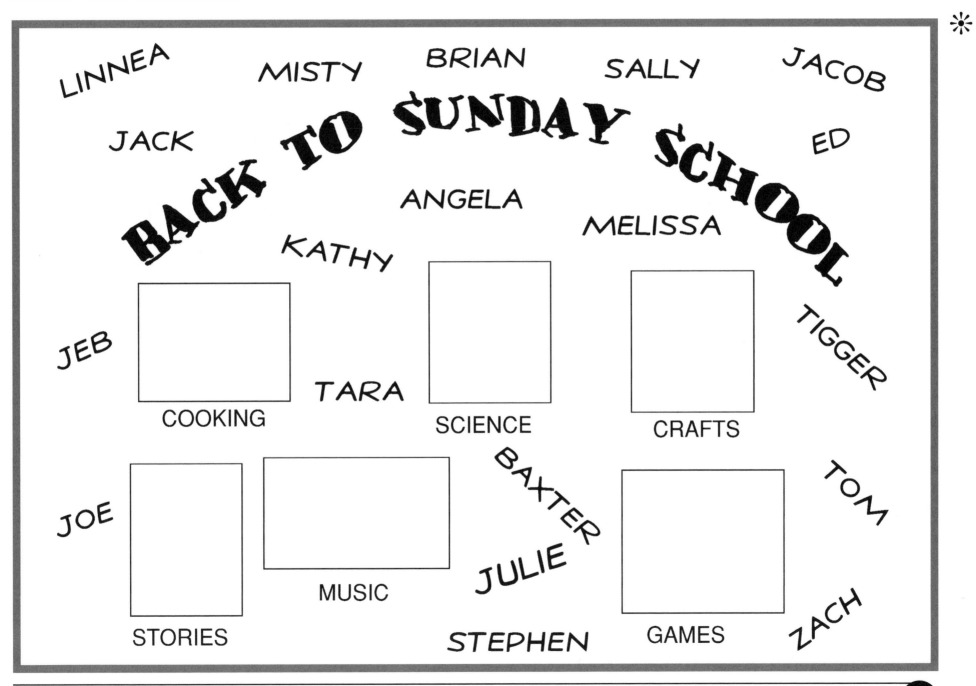

OCTOBER

KEY SCRIPTURE VERSE

Genesis 1:24: "And God said, 'Let the earth bring forth living creatures of every kind.'"

BLESSING OF THE ANIMALS SERVICE

Invite church members to bring their pets to church for a "Blessing of the Animals Service" in honor of St. Francis of Assisi. Use scripture readings, music, and more to make this a special time for the pets of your congregation. Look up St. Francis of Assisi and Blessing of the Animals on the Internet for information on creating this special service.

OCTOBER SERVICE PROJECT: FOR OUR FURRY FRIENDS

Ask people to donate new pet supplies (food, toys, dishes) and give these to a local pet shelter.

OCTOBER BULLETIN BOARD: MEET OUR PETS

MATERIALS
Green paper to cover the board
Letter stencils (use a die-cutting machine if available)
Pushpins
Bright yellow cardstock paper

PREPARATION
- Cover the board with green paper.
- Cut the title out of the yellow paper and attach it to the board.

DIRECTIONS
- Ask members of the congregation to bring photos of their pets and attach them to the board.

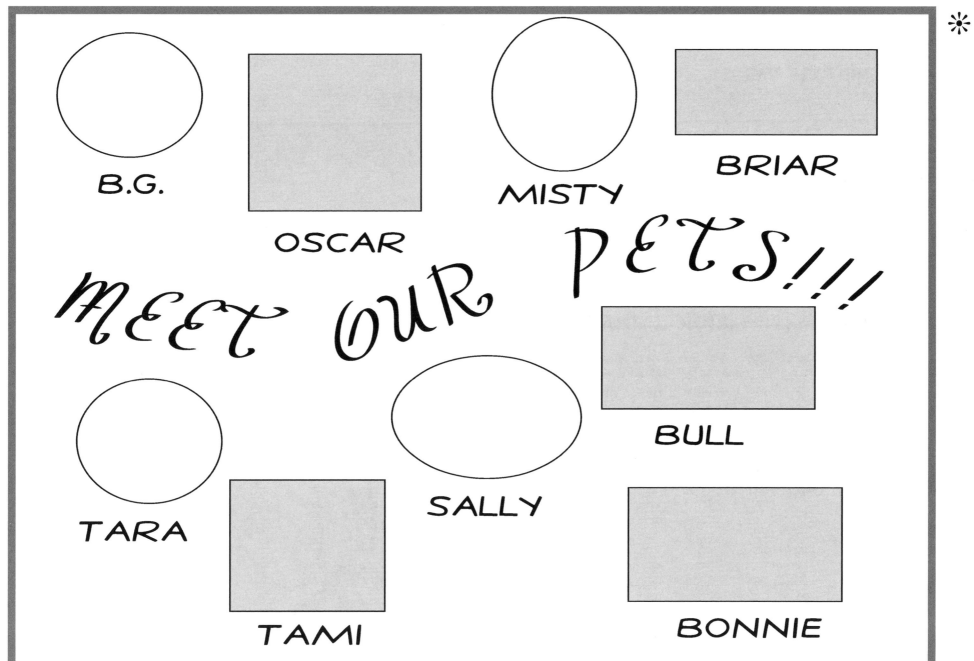

NOVEMBER

KEY SCRIPTURE VERSE

Psalm 67:7: "May God continue to bless us;
let all the ends of the earth revere him."

SCHOOL'S OUT VACATION BIBLE SCHOOL

Choose a theme and plan a one-day vacation Bible school for the Friday after Thanksgiving. See my other books for ideas. This can be a lead-in to your annual Advent activities. Consider offering similar programs on other school holidays or during winter and spring breaks.

NOVEMBER SERVICE PROJECT: THANK YOU

Use white paper, crayons, markers, and stickers to create original thank-you cards that will be delivered to local community agencies (fire department, police department, hospitals, public library, public works department). Mail these to the appropriate agency.

NOVEMBER BULLETIN BOARD: OVERFLOWING WITH GOD'S BLESSINGS

MATERIALS

Yellow paper to cover the board
Large 3-D cornucopia
Red and orange paper
Black markers
Pushpins and heavy-duty long T-tacks
Letter stencils (use a die-cutting machine if available)

PREPARATION

- Cover the board with yellow paper.
- Cut the title out of the orange paper and attach it to the board.
- Attach the cornucopia to the board.
- Cut out leaves from red and orange paper.

DIRECTIONS

- Give each person a leaf and a black marker. Ask each person to write a blessing on the leaf and attach it to the board so the leaves spill out of the cornucopia.

Adjust size
as needed

OVERFLOWING ... WITH GOD'S BLESSINGS

FOOD
CHURCH
FAMILY
GRACE
LOVE
GOOD HEALTH

DECEMBER

KEY SCRIPTURE VERSE

Isaiah 9:6: "For a child has been born for us; a son given to us."

CRAFT CORNER CAMP

Provide a variety of easy-to-make Christmas and winter crafts. Oriental Trading Company has many of these at nominal prices. See page 145 for information. Let every person make one craft to keep and one to give as a gift.

DECEMBER SERVICE PROJECT: A GIFT FOR YOU

Give the extra crafts people made at Craft Corner Camp to those people in your congregation who are hospitalized or homebound for Christmas.

DECEMBER BULLETIN BOARD: WE ARE PART OF CHRIST'S CIRCLE OF LOVE

MATERIALS

Shiny gold Christmas wrapping paper to cover the board
Shiny red Christmas wrapping paper
Green cardstock paper
Pencils
Scissors
Pushpins
Photos of members of your congregation (take instant photos or have people bring one)
Letter stencils (use a die-cutting machine if available)

PREPARATION
- Cover the board with the shiny gold paper.
- Cut out the title from the shiny red paper and attach it to the board.

DIRECTIONS
- Give each person a piece of green paper and a pencil. Let them trace their hands onto the green cardstock paper and cut them out.
- Attach the green handprints to the board so they form a wreath.
- Attach the photographs to the board so they are in the center of the wreath.

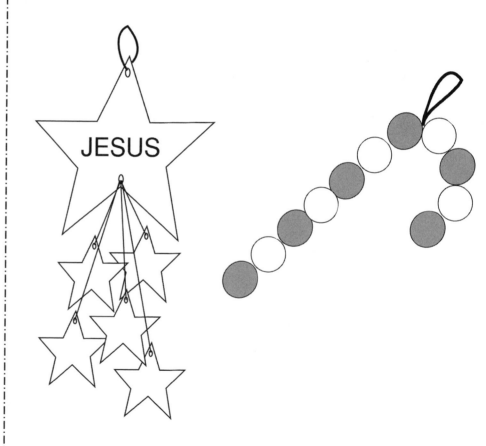

Section Five

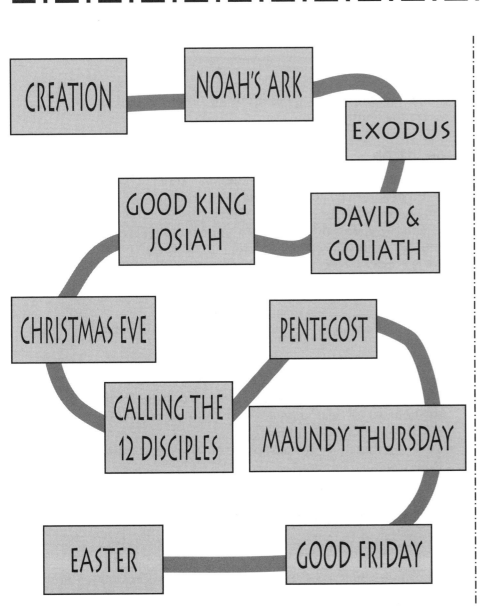

CREATION

NOAH'S ARK

EXODUS

GOOD KING JOSIAH

DAVID & GOLIATH

CHRISTMAS EVE

PENTECOST

CALLING THE 12 DISCIPLES

MAUNDY THURSDAY

EASTER

GOOD FRIDAY

BIBLE ACTIVITIES

The ideas featured here include activities that will encourage people to visit your church and encourage them to attend your Christian education programs and worship services. These activities encourage church members of all ages to participate and work together. Use these activities *after* you have shared several of the lessons in the book.

THE BIBLE STORY TIME LINE

This activity can be used in connection with the stories and activities in all of my books. This will include your entire Christian education program from preschool through high school and adult classes. This is going to become an all-church event, so begin planning and preparing early. Begin making the games several weeks in advance. Set this up the evening prior to the program and ask for help from adult volunteers.

Plan to do this on a Saturday and invite the entire community to your church to enjoy your Bible Story Time Line. If necessary, charge a fee per person to cover the cost of the program.

You might have to use all areas of your fellowship hall, hallways, and classrooms to accommodate the Bible Story Time Line.

Begin with the story of the Creation, and go all the way through the Bible as you create a Bible Story Time Line. Set up a table for each story you choose to highlight. Let each class of children, youth, and adults be responsible for a different Bible story. Invite each church committee to help with a Bible Story Time Line.

Also plan to invite people to the sanctuary throughout the day to watch videos of Bible stories and enjoy sing-alongs.

On the day of the program have volunteers wear biblical costumes (see p. xii). Those portraying characters from the stories highlighted can be at the table that features that story. Let other members dress as Bible citizens who will wander about the area visiting with guests. Let all children attending the Bible Story Time Line don tunics. These can be easily made by folding a 3' x 3' or larger square of material in half corner-to-corner. Cut an opening in the middle, so the tunic can slip over the child's head.

LINE TABLES

Include books, artwork, music, games, and props that you have created and shared in your study of that Bible story. Include crafts people can do and foods they can taste at the various tables.

For example: let kids glue white cotton clouds and a sunshine sticker to a piece of blue paper at the "Creation" table. Have goldfish crackers and bread to nibble on at the "Fishes and Loaves" table. Have puzzles of some of the Bible stories at other tables. Set up "fun fair" types of games (ring toss, fishing, bowling) at the different stations.

The tables should be set up in biblical order so that those attending can learn the stories in the order they occur in the Bible. Post the dates each story occurred on the wall behind each table.

BIBLE VARIETY SHOW

Plan a Bible Variety Show where children and adults sing songs, present puppet shows, tell stories, and present skits based on the Bible stories they have learned in my series of books. Let individuals, small groups, and the entire Sunday school population participate. Children and adults can form groups to present a variety of skits based on Bible stories. Other groups can sing some of the songs in this book. Some people might be willing to sing or play instrumental solos. Teach several songs to *all* of the children and let them present that as a finale. Let them release helium-filled balloons and toss out confetti and streamers at the end.

Decorate the room with artwork done by the children. Serve refreshments based on the stories in my books.

BIBLE SCAVENGER HUNT

The children will need to read and decipher each clue to determine what objects they must find. The children can find the items on the list by visiting neighboring houses to ask for the objects or by looking for objects that are hidden throughout your building.

Found items can include actual objects or pictures of the objects. If you do this activity in your building, it will be much easier to use actual objects. Decide which method works best for your situation. The clues and objects to be found are based on Bible stories in this book. The adults accompanying the children should encourage the children to decipher the clues on their own rather than doing it for them.

MATERIALS

One large brown paper bag per group of 4 to 6 children
Prizes for the winning team

PREPARATION

- Look at the suggested hints below under "Scavenger Hunt Answers." Create additional hints as desired.
- Prepare one list for each group.
- If you are doing this activity in your building, you will need to hide all of the objects the children are to find. You can also vary each list so each group is looking for different items.

DIRECTIONS

- Divide the children into groups of 4 to 6 accompanied by 1 or 2 adults.
- Tell the children that they must decipher all of the clues to determine what objects they must find on the hunt.
- Explain to the children that they will need to ask for these items at the homes they visit in your neighborhood or look for them hidden throughout your building.
- The team that finds the most objects in the shortest amount of time is declared the winner.

SCAVENGER HUNT ANSWERS

Bricks, Basket, Stones, Lamb, Crown, Lions, Christmas Tree, Candy Cane, Wreath, Angel, Star, Wise Men, Donkey, Money Changers, Pray, Two Coins, Garden, Nailed, Jesus

THE GREAT AND WONDERFUL BIBLE STORY SCAVENGER HUNT

Decipher the clues, and find items that represent each answer.

1. The people used ___ ___ ___ ___ ___ ___ to build the Tower of Babel.

2. Moses' mother put him into a ___ ___ ___ ___ ___ ___ and hid him in the bulrushes.

3. David used ___ ___ ___ ___ ___ ___ to slay Goliath.

4. The wolf shall live with the ___ ___ ___ ___.

5. King Josiah wore a ___ ___ ___ ___ ___ on his head.

6. Daniel was afraid the ___ ___ ___ ___ ___ might eat him after he was thrown into their den.

7. The ___ ___ ___ ___ ___ ___ ___ ___ ___ ___ ___ ___ ___ points to heaven to remind us that Jesus lives there.

8. The ___ ___ ___ ___ ___ ___ ___ ___ ___ reminds us of a shepherd's staff or it can be the letter "J" in Jesus' name.

9. The ___ ___ ___ ___ ___ ___ is shaped like a circle to remind us that we are surrounded by God's circle of love.

10. An ___ ___ ___ ___ ___ told Mary that she would be the mother of God's son.

11. A ___ ___ ___ ___ shined in the sky the night Jesus was born.

12. The ___ ___ ___ ___ ___ ___ ___ brought gifts when they came to visit Jesus.

13. Jesus rode a ___ ___ ___ ___ ___ ___ on Palm Sunday.

14. Jesus was angry at the ___ ___ ___ ___ ___ ___ ___ ___ ___ ___ ___ ___ in the temple.

15. Jesus wants us to ___ ___ ___ ___ every day.

16. The widow gave ___ ___ ___ ___ ___ ___ ___ to the temple.

17. Jesus prayed in the ___ ___ ___ ___ ___ ___ after he had celebrated Passover with his disciples.

18. Jesus was ___ ___ ___ ___ ___ ___ to the cross to be crucified.

19. ___ ___ ___ ___ ___ was resurrected from the dead.

BIBLE STORY ART

Here are three art projects that highlight the stories in this book. Complete these projects *after* you have enjoyed all of the stories in the book.

YOUR CHURCH'S BIBLE ART GALLERY

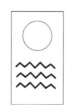

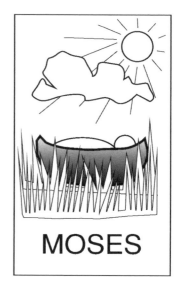

MATERIALS

Two sheets of 8" x 10" white cardstock paper per child
Crayons, colored markers, glitter pens
One inexpensive picture frame with glass per child
Picture hangers and hooks for each frame
A medium-sized container
Typed title of each Bible story you choose to use
Camera and film
Lined paper and pencils
Computer, printer, disk
Laminating machine and film or clear contact paper

PREPARATION

- Select an area in your church that can become a permanent Bible Art Gallery for displaying children's Bible artwork. Create an attractive, eye-catching sign that says: "(Church Name) Bible Art Gallery. The artwork here was designed and donated by the children in our Sunday school."

DIRECTIONS

- Type up a list of the Bible stories in this book. Cut the titles out and place them into the container.
- Let each child reach into the container and pull out a Bible story title.
- Have each child use the crayons, markers, and glitter markers to illustrate the story they chose. Tell the kids to

neatly print the title of the story somewhere on the picture so it is easily read. Let each child autograph (first and last name) the bottom of their picture in the lower left corner. Give the pictures plenty of time to dry, especially if the children have used glitter pens.

- Take a color photo of each child holding up their finished picture. Let each child write a paragraph telling about themselves (name, age, grade, interests).
- Once the pictures are dry, frame them and hang them on the wall in the gallery.
- Type up each child's paragraph. Cut the paragraph out of the paper and glue it to the bottom half of a piece of white cardstock paper. Glue the child's photo above it. Attach this to the wall next to each child's original artwork.
- Take photos of this gallery and add them to your church's website.

YOUR CHURCH'S ILLUSTRATED BOOK OF BIBLE STORIES

Choose the Bible stories you wish to include in your book. Type up a one-page, condensed version of each Bible story chosen. Let the children choose a Bible story from the ones that you provide. Each child will illustrate the Bible story they choose. Let each child sign their name at the bottom of their illustration. Put the printed stories and illustrations into plastic sleeves, making sure the story and illustration face each other. Arrange them into biblical order. Put the plastic sleeves into a binder that has a plastic cover on the front. Ask someone to design an attractive cover for your book and slide the picture into the plastic cover. Catalog the book and put it into your church library. Mention this newest addition to your church library in your church newsletter.

FAITH CHURCH'S ILLUSTRATED BOOK OF BIBLE STORIES

BIBLE ART GREETING CARDS

Give each child an 8½" x 5½" piece of white cardstock paper that is folded in half. Let the kids draw a picture of their favorite Bible story on the front of the card. On the inside, they can write a greeting to their parents. Put the cards into envelopes and mail them to each child's home. Make sure that children who come from separated families create cards to send to both homes.

BIBLE STORY GAMES

The three games featured here highlight the Bible stories in this book. Play these games *after* you have enjoyed the stories. The games will help children remember each Bible story.

BIBLE BUCKET BIBLE STORIES

MATERIALS

One empty ice-cream bucket per Bible story
Contact paper in a variety of colors and patterns
Beanbags
Three objects that highlight each Bible story (for example, Daniel in the Lions' Den could include a small toy lion, a plastic toy boy, and an angel. The story of Christmas would include a diaper, a star, and a baby toy)
One typed and laminated title for each story
Masking tape
Laminating machine and film or clear contact paper

PREPARATION

• Cover each bucket with a different color or pattern of contact paper.
• Tape a title of a story to the bottom of each bucket.
• Arrange the buckets on the floor so they are spaced one right next to the other in a square formation.
• Attach a masking tape line to the floor.

DIRECTIONS

• Have each child take a turn standing behind the line and tossing the beanbag into a bucket.
• When the beanbag lands in a bucket, remove the three items from the bucket, show them to the child, and ask if the child can identify the story.
• See if the children can briefly tell you the story in their own words.
• Play until all of the stories have been revealed.

HINT: If necessary, offer a choice of three stories for younger kids—"Would you find these in Daniel in the Lions' Den, Moses in the Bulrushes, or the Story of Jesus' Birth?"

THE BIBLE COVER-UP GAME

MATERIALS

White 8" x 12" cardstock paper
Color copier
One color illustration from each Bible story in this book
Colored markers, glue sticks, scissors
Laminating machine and film or clear contact paper

PREPARATION

- Color copy a picture from each Bible story.
- Glue each picture to a piece of cardstock paper.
- Print the title of each Bible story on the back of each picture. Print 3 words that identify that story on the back of each picture. For example, for Daniel in the Lions' Den, you might print "lions, angel, brave."
- Laminate each picture.
- Arrange the pictures in a stack so they are in random order.

DIRECTIONS

- Show each picture and read the words on the back of each card. See if the kids can identify each story.

CROWNED HEADS OF THE BIBLE

MATERIALS

One color picture or word clues from each Bible story
White cardstock paper
Glue sticks, masking tape, colored markers
Laminating machine and film or clear contact paper
CD player and CD of lively Christian kids songs
One inexpensive gold, paper crown per child (found in party stores)

PREPARATION

- Glue each picture to a piece of cardstock paper.
- Laminate each card.

- Place each card face down on the floor.
- Set aside a "Crowned Heads of the Bible" area. Make a large sign that says, CROWNED HEADS OF THE BIBLE and tape it to the wall.

DIRECTIONS

- Have each child stand on a card.
- Play the music. Tell the kids to walk around the room. When the music stops, each child must find a card to stand on.
- When you stop the music, call on a child. Ask that child to pick up the card, he or she is standing on and show it to the others. See if that child can identify which Bible story the picture depicts.
- If correct, the child receives his or her crown and moves over to the "Crowned Heads of the Bible" area. If not, the card goes back on the floor, and the child remains in the game.
- Keep playing until all of the kids become "Crowned Heads of the Bible."
- Take a photo of the "Crowned Heads of the Bible," and post it on your church website. Let the kids keep their crowns.

IDEAS

- You can also do this using three word clues from each story rather than pictures.
- To make the game more challenging have two cards per story, one with word clues and one with pictures.

Bibliography

Around the Christmas Tree. Milwaukee: Hal Leonard Corp., 1995.
  Includes: "Hark! The Herald Angels Sing," "Love Came Down at Christmas," and "O Christmas Tree."
Auld, Mary. *Daniel in the Lions' Den*. New York: Franklin Watts, 1999.
  Daniel's faith in God helped him while he was in a den of lions.
———. *David and Goliath*. New York: Franklin Watts, 1999.
  David bravely fought the giant Goliath.
———. *Moses in the Bulrushes*. New York: Franklin Watts, 1999.
  Moses' mother put him in a basket and let him float away so she could save him from death.
Benagh, Christine L. *Daniel and the Lions' Den*. Nashville: Abingdon Press, 1986.
  Daniel bravely stayed with the lions and wasn't harmed.
The Best Hymns Ever. Milwaukee: Hal Leonard, 2002.
  Includes: "Christ the Lord Is Risen Today."
Brown, Margaret Wise. *A Child Is Born*. New York: Jump at the Sun, 2000.
  A very special baby was born one night in Bethlehem.
Day-Bivins, Pat, and Philip Dale Smith. *The Rabbit and the Promise Sign*. Tacoma: Golden Anchor, 1998.
  A young rabbit stays awake with Jesus while he is in the Garden of Gethsemane.
dePaola, Tomie. *The Legend of Old Befana*. New York: Harcourt Brace and Company, 1980.
  Old Befana was too busy to take time to join the people going to see a newborn King!
de Regniers, Beatrice Schenk. *David and Goliath*. New York: Orchard Books, 1993.
  David bravely fought off a giant!
Dingwall, Cindy. *Bible Banquets with Kids: 20 Scripture-based Celebrations to Share with Children*. Nashville: Abingdon, 2000.
  A bounty of Bible stories that feature food are highlighted through storytelling, games, music, crafts, and, of course, eating!
———. *Bible Time with Kids: 400+ Bible-based Activities to Use with Children*. Nashville: Abingdon, 1997.
  Story sharing, games, movement, crafts, music, puppetry, and more bring Bible stories to life.
———. *Bible Verse Fun with Kids: 200+ Ideas and Activities that Help Children Learn and Live Scripture*. Nashville: Abingdon, 2004.
  Children will learn and remember twenty-five Bible verses as they explore them through games, movement, story sharing, music, crafts, and more.
———. *Give Thanks! Anytime Activities*. Grand Rapids: In Celebration, 2000.
  Scripture-based puzzles and activities about giving thanks.
———. *God Created Animals*. Grand Rapids: In Celebration, 1999.
  Scripture-based activities about animals.
———. *Happy Birthday, America!* Fort Atkinson, Wis.: Alleyside Press, 2000.
  Celebrate the birth of America and some of her famous people with creative and innovative activities.

———. *Jesus Lives*. Grand Rapids: In Celebration, 1999.
  Activities about Jesus.
———. *Library Celebrations*. Fort Atkinson, Wis.: Alleyside Press, 1999.
  Celebrate libraries and other important library events such as Children's Book Week, National Library Week, and more through storytelling and other enjoyable activities.
———. *Storybook Birthday Parties*. Fort Atkinson, Wis.: Alleyside Press, 1998.
  Celebrate the birthdays of favorite book characters with stories, music, games, prizes, and more!
———. *Words to Live By: Bible Verse Rebuses*. Grand Rapids: In Celebration, 2000.
  Rebus puzzles highlight Bible verses.
———. *Worship Time with Kids: Bible-based Activities for Children's Church*. Nashville: Abingdon, 1998.
  Children will delight in the Lord as they worship God through songs, games, stories, children's messages, crafts, and other activities.
Fox, Dan. *We Wish You a Merry Christmas: Songs of the Season for Young People*. New York: Metropolitan Museum of Art, 1989.
  Includes: "Hark! The Herald Angels Sing" and "O Christmas Tree."
Glatzer, Jenna. *Hattie, Get a Haircut!* New York: Moo Press, 2005.
  Hattie is afraid to get a haircut. When she finally agrees that she does indeed need one, she donates her hair to an organization that makes wigs for children who have lost their hair.
Goldstein, Ernest. *Edward Hicks' The Peaceable Kingdom*. Champaign, Ill.: Garrard Publishing Company, 1982.
  Contains information about the various paintings of "The Peaceable Kingdom" by Edward Hicks.
Haidle, Helen. *He Is Alive!* Grand Rapids: Zonderkids, 2001.
  A collection of short stories highlight the final week of Jesus and the resurrection.
Heyer, Carol. *The Easter Story*. Nashville: Ideals, 1990.
  This book focuses on the events of holy week and ends with the resurrection of Jesus.
Hirsh, Marilyn. *The Tower of Babel*. New York: Holiday House, 1981.
  The people used their pride to build a tower to honor themselves rather than to honor God.
Larcombe, Jennifer Rees. *The Baby in the Basket*. Wheaton, Ill.: Crossway Books, 1999.
  Moses was saved for a very special purpose.
Leisy, James F. *The Good Times Music Songbook*. Wheaton, Ill.: Crossway Books, 1999.
  Includes: "Hark! The Herald Angels Sing" and "O Christmas Tree."
The Life Application Bible. Iowa Falls: World Bible Publishers, 1989.
  Includes the full Bible with commentaries, biographical listings, tables, charts, and provides insight and understanding to biblical texts.
Maccarone, Grace. *A Child Was Born*. New York: Scholastic, 2000.
  The birth of Jesus is told in rhyme.

McCarthy, Michael. *The Story of Daniel in the Lions' Den*. Cambridge, Mass.: Barefoot Books, 2003.
> Daniel bravely spent the night in a den of hungry lions!

McGee, Marni. *The Colt and the King*. New York, Holiday House, 2002.
> A colt tells how he carried Jesus during the Palm Sunday parade.

Novak, Matt. *Mr. Floop's Lunch*. London: Orchard Books, 1990.

Osborne, Rick. *The Legend of the Christmas Tree*. Grand Rapids, Zonderkids, 2001.
> A family learns about Christmas trees as they search for the perfect tree for their home. *(Also available as a shortened version board book.)*

Pingry, Patricia A. *A Child's Easter*. Candy Cane Press/Ideas, 2001.
> A young child meets Jesus and watches his final week on earth, and then witnesses the resurrection.

The Praise and Worship Fake Book. Milwaukee: Hal Leonard, 2004.
> Includes: "Spirit Song."

Taylor, Shirley. *The Cross in the Egg*. Little Rock: August House, 1999.
> One of the eggs has a crack shaped like a cross.

Walburg, Lori. *The Legend of the Candy Cane*. Grand Rapids: Zondervan, 1997.
> A young girl learns about the candy cane.

Zadrzynska, Ewa. *The Peaceable Kingdom*. New York: M.M. Art Books, 1993.
> What an exciting adventure these animals had!

Suppliers Guide

Betty Lukens Felt Figures
711 Portal Street
Cotati, CA 94931
1-800-541-9279
www.bettylukens.com
Beautiful flannel board Bible stories and scenery that are well worth purchasing.

Folkmanis Puppets
Puppets on the Pier
Pier 39 Space H-4
San Francisco, CA 94133
1-800-443-4463
www.folkmanis.com
A wide variety of puppets that can be used for Bible-based puppet shows.

Homespun Kids
P.O. Box 1075
Fall City, WA 98024
www.homespunkids.com
Includes beautiful flannel boards and other aids for teaching Bible stories.

Lakeshore Learning Materials
2695 E. Dominguez Street
Carson, CA 90895
1-800-428-4414
www.lakeshorelearning.com
A vast variety of educational materials, displays, bulletin boards, puzzles, props, and more.

Oriental Trading Company
P.O. Box 2308
Omaha, NE 68103-2308
1-800-875-8480
www.orientaltrading.com
Includes crafts, prizes, and more at reasonable prices.

S & S Worldwide
75 Mill Street
Colchester, CT 06414
1-800-243-9232
www.ssww.com
Includes crafts at reasonable prices.

 Scripture Index

Author, Title, Subject Index